American Catholic Crossroads

By Walter J. Ong, S.J.

Frontiers in American Catholicism
Essays on Ideology and Culture

American Catholic Crossroads
*Religious-Secular Encounters
in the Modern World*

Ramus, Method, and the Decay of Dialogue
*From the Art of Discourse to
the Art of Reason*

Ramus and Talon Inventory

American Catholic Crossroads
Religious-Secular Encounters in the Modern World

Walter J. Ong, S.J.

New York
THE MACMILLAN COMPANY
1959

Imprimi potest
Joseph P. Fisher, S.J.
Provincial, Missouri Province
St. Louis, Missouri, September 24, 1958

Imprimatur
✠ Joseph E. Ritter
Archbishop of St. Louis
October 10, 1958

© Walter J. Ong 1959

All rights reserved—no part of this book may be reproduced in any form without permission in writing from the publisher, except by a reviewer who wishes to quote brief passages in connection with a review written for inclusion in magazine or newspaper.

First Printing

The Macmillan Company, New York
Brett-Macmillan Ltd., Galt, Ontario

Printed in the United States of America

For permission to use, generally in revised form, material from previously published essays, grateful acknowledgment is hereby made to the holders of the original copyrights. These essays are: "Religious-Secular Dialogue in a Pluralist Society" which was a lecture at the Seminar on Religion in a Free Society sponsored by the Fund for the Republic in May, 1958, in New York City and subsequently was printed in a symposium entitled *Religion in America*, edited by John Cogley, copyright 1958 Meridian Books, Inc.; and "Secular Knowledge and Revealed Religion" which appeared in *Religious Education* (LII, 5, p. 341), copyright 1957 Religious Education Association (New York City).

Library of Congress catalog card number: 59-7973

For my brother Richard,
his wife Mary,
and their children
Richard and Barbara

Preface
TWO CITIES

One of the classic formulations of the position of the Christian in the world is that of St. Augustine's City of God and City of Man. In the case of a mind as supple and profound as St. Augustine's, sensitive to the claims of history beyond his age and certainly beyond the ages which immediately followed him, one would think that this formulation would bring him to speak of the relation of the Redemption to the entire cosmos. Strangely enough, he does not find the occasion to do so—in *The City of God* or elsewhere. Fearful of the concupiscence of the flesh and of the eyes and of the pride of life which makes "the world" for which Jesus says He does not pray, St. Augustine shies away from the natural world itself.

His vision falls short of a vision of cosmic salvation, as Henri Irénée Marrou has pointed out in his *St. Augustine and His Influence Through the Ages*. The Christian is in the natural world, St. Augustine admits, but, unlike most of the Greek Fathers of the Church and unlike St. Paul, who speaks of the "eager longing of creation" which has been "groaning in travail together until now," this greatest of the Western Fathers shies away from considering anything but man as redeemable. His shying away appears to have at least two causes. He feared his old Manicheism which had taught that matter was evil: to think of the cosmos as a whole as somehow redeemable (through man, redeemed by Christ) would hint that what was material was after all of itself bad. Alongside this was an ingrained suspicion of the material universe as seductive to fallen man, a suspicion less than Manichean and, in fact, very well grounded. St. Augustine seems to have decided, or to have drifted into, the policy of letting the natural material universe alone. His concern with history, which would seem to throw him into the maelstrom of this universe, turns on the history of the individual human being, the microcosm rather than the macrocosm, and the relationship of the microcosm to God, to the neglect of the history of the universe in which the human species appears. His historicism has the limitations of that of many approaches qualified today as existentialist: rich in its insights into the problems of the individual, it shies away from thought of the human individual as a phenomenon appearing at the culmination of a tremendous cosmic development.

The Augustinian heritage is very much present in the United States and was particularly strong in our seventeenth century Puritan tradition, where its features have been anatomized by Perry Miller and others. But there is also a trend of thought among both American Protestants and Catholics which makes them take a more positive view of the material cosmos than St. Augustine had. Indeed, this trend of thought is characteristic of much, if not most, present-day manifestations of the Christian tradition. It is in great part derivative from the Middle Ages where, in addition to an otherworldly outlook which remained relatively firm, a tradition of studying logic and physics far stronger than the ancient world had known worked with other factors to build up a more positive attitude toward the natural sciences than early man generally had enjoyed. Greater familiarity with the material cosmos has brought greater respect for it and a greater willingness, on the part of many religious persons, to think of it, and indeed to meditate religiously on the details which we now know of its mysteries. We must always remember that back of the Augustinian shyness with regard to the material universe lay a great chaos of ignorance. Greek civilization was less ignorant than Latin, and the Greek Fathers correspondingly took the view just mentioned, rather less negative regarding the material cosmos than St. Augustine's. But the material cosmos did not belong to man, Greek or Latin, so effectively and thoroughly in earlier ages as it does now in our technological civilization.

In the development of a greater respect for the material cosmos, Christianity has been at least a collaborator, particularly in the Catholic Church, with her straightforward teachings regarding the Incarnation, regarding the importance of the Mother of God (who gave Jesus Christ His body), regarding the sacraments, which bring God and His grace into intimate relationship with the material here-and-now, and especially regarding the Holy Eucharist, the sacrament of sacraments, where the relationship of Jesus Christ, Who is God, to the here and now is most spectacularly shown forth. But besides this nuclear effect of Christianity radiating out continuously from within the bosom of the Church, there is a kind of diffused effect which operates in areas as far afield as Marxism. For if the Marxist interpretation of history is a far cry from the Christian interpretation, the Marxist enthusiasm for history is a product of the Christian milieu.

The themes of the present essays have to do with various aspects of the relationship between the Catholic tradition and the secular world in the United States of America. In a sense this relationship poses old problems, the most basic one that of nature and grace. But in another sense the problems are not old at all, but new and fresh, for the universe in which they are being posed is manifestly changing before our eyes and changing with somewhat more than deliberate speed.

Of course, the relationship between the City of God and the City of Man is in certain ways what it was in St. Augustine's day. The City of God should be our dominant concern. The City of Man holds the threat of sin. But our knowledge of the material universe in which the City of Man comes into being is incredibly more detailed and accurate than it was in the early Christian era. It is not complete, of course, and never will be. But it is enlarged enough to encourage our rethinking of questions concerning God's Providence in His universe. These questions touch not only the material universe but the universe of intelligence itself which is born into the material world with man, for we know now to some extent the tremendous development which man's fund of knowledge and ways of approaching the being around him undergoes over the centuries and millennia. Finally, our growing knowledge of the material cosmos invites us to deepen our understanding of what the term Catholic itself may mean.

Contents

Preface	TWO CITIES	vii
1	THE CHURCH AND COSMIC HISTORY	1
2	RELIGIOUS-SECULAR DIALOGUE IN A PLURALIST SOCIETY	16
3	FATHER HECKER AND THE AMERICAN SITUATION	46
4	SECULAR KNOWLEDGE AND REVEALED RELIGION	67
5	RESEARCH AND AMERICAN CATHOLIC EDUCATION	91
6	THE APOSTOLATE OF SECULAR ARTS AND SCIENCES	118
	INDEX	157

1
The Church and Cosmic History

Within the past few generations historical awareness has grown among Catholics as among other men. Catholics have become sensible not only of the cultural advantages of knowing history as an agglomerate of more or less interesting facts but also of the need to think of the Church herself, as well as divine revelation in the Scriptures and in tradition, within a historical context. There is no revelation outside history, and no Church either.

The full implications involved in our new awareness are still being worked out as it becomes more and more apparent that religious sensitivity to history and to its claims is peculiarly congenial to the Hebraic and Christian tradition in a way in which it is to none other. In *The Myth of the Eternal Return* Mircea Eliade has pointed out in fascinating and profound anthropological and psychological detail how pagan mythologizing and pagan philosophizing about the cosmos and time are essentially a flight from history. Although the germ of a historical outlook is inseparable from Christian revelation, mankind's delay through previous Christian ages in developing what is now regarded as a normal historical sense would thus appear as a residue of paganism—a residue which, as Eliade's book makes quite evident, persists in patterns of thought and speech and behavior even in the most anciently Catholic civilizations.

The individual man may accept Christ and His Church and be thereby redeemed, but the penetration of Christianity into the common store of knowledge by which man lives his natural life takes generations and presumably will never be complete until the end of time. For the store of knowledge by which an individual lives is not all his, nor under his control. The bits of knowledge in his mind are only points of contact with the great store of knowledge present in the culture which has formed him and preserved by the peculiar developments of the culture's language and institutions. And all human cultures have pagan roots. None can fully qualify as Catholic.

In part the penetration of Christianity into culture depends on the evolution of human society itself and on the greater control of the material universe and the greater degree of awareness which comes with this evolution. The disregard for the individual which marks many primitive societies militates against the Christian notion of personal responsibility if not, at times, even against the Christian notion of the value of human life. It is certain that concern about the personal as against the social effects of sin was much less developed in earlier Christian civilizations, living a marginal material existence, than it has been in the West since the first signs of our present economy of abundance began to appear around the sixteenth century.

The development of a sense of history itself depends on the development of human society in history. For it was impossible to feel about history as acutely as we feel today, and thus impossible effectively to feel the Church in history, until systems of communication and of scientific investigation had themselves developed to the point where large stores of knowledge about natural reality could be accumulated and to some degree organized.

Once human history develops to the point where history itself becomes a burning concern of man, something like a new dimension is given to nature itself. The quest of nature or natures is the quest of beginnings—*natura* in Latin means primarily birth, and the term developed its present meaning *because* it had this meaning of birth. Nature is sometimes defined as the principle of operation in things—but this is also to say the starting point or beginning of operation in things, for a principle or *principium* is a "first" or a "beginning." When this world of nature or of beginnings develops a knowledge of its own temporal beginnings, as it does now that man, the most striking phenomenon in the world of nature, has accumulated real knowledge about the past ages of the cosmos, we have a world in which nature itself is reflexive in a new and urgent way.

At this point the old logion "Grace builds on nature" is seen to have richer implications than before. As the Incarnation penetrates natural reality through the Church, the process of penetration involves not merely the extension of the effects of the Incarnation to more and more individuals—a kind of numerical extension—but an internal unfolding comparable to that of a fertilized germ cell as it builds itself through successive embryonic and fetal stages into the adult organism. Has not Christ compared His Church precisely to this sort of thing, a germinal organism, a grain of wheat, a mustard seed? As human nature becomes more and more reflexively aware of itself and of its historical place in a historical cosmos, which through history has arrived at the point where the study of history becomes not merely a possibility but indeed the passion of thinking man, the Church herself becomes more aware of herself in relation to mankind. Indeed, it appears that, as time goes on, she will always know more and more about herself in this relationship, for, through a continuously growing geology and astronomy and anthropology and linguistics and psychology, mankind continues to know more and more of its own natural past and its relationship to the cosmos.

Since the Church is unequivocally committed to history by the historical fact of the Incarnation, a lack of historical perspective which is disastrous philosophically is doubly disastrous when we approach the realm of revelation. To apply to the economy of revelation the Platonic philosophy of "ideas," suggesting that there is somewhere or somehow an "idea" of revelation or an "idea" of the Church which is perfect because divorced from the material universe, would seem to be not only philosophically shortsighted and useless, but also quite heretical. For the Church stems from Christ Incarnate, Who is very much in the material universe, and, in His human nature, of it.

Aristotelian types of a-historicism are hardly less objectionable than the Platonic. Aristotle maintains, for example, in his *Art of Poetry,* that poetry is superior to history in that it represents the universal and history the particular. Present-day poetic theory, while not unaware of the sense in which Aristotle's statement is true (poetry, as such, is certainly not concerned with the individual in the historical sense), does not find this statement of the case very adequate, for such a statement underrates the particularity of poetry, of which our historical age is intensely aware. But the Christian today demurs still more strongly. This unqualified endorsement of the superiority of the universal to the particular does not sit well with him at all. For revelation comes to us not in "universals"—even the "universals" of the Greek poetic myths—but through precisely a historical Person, Jesus Christ, Who is Himself unique, not universal, and yet is the Exemplar of all things, and for Whom a long history of a special historical people, the Hebrews, was the foreshadowing preparation.

Thus our present historical sensitivity has made more than ever evident the fact that the Incarnation, in which God took to Himself the contingent and thereby elevated historical contingency to a more-than-universality, is a scandal to the fundamental a-historicism of both Plato and Aristotle and of the Gentiles over the entire surface of the earth. St. Paul well knew of this scandal. We can feel some of the reasons for it more acutely today.

II

If Catholics today have some awareness of the importance of history, this does not mean that Catholics' views of history do not at times leave much to be desired. Catholics may curtail their view of history if only because some of the consequences of the historicity of the Redemption may leave even some Catholics uncomfortable. We can be taken aback by a statement of the historicity of the Redemption so blunt as that of Gerard Manley Hopkins when, in *The Wreck of the Deutschland,* he says of grace that it does not come straight from heaven—"Not out of His bliss." This seems somehow vaguely derogatory of God, and more particularly of His majesty. Yet it is true, for, as Hopkins goes on, all grace "dates" from the year of the Incarnation, from a certain definite time in the history of the cosmos, wherein grace is mysteriously lodged through the Incarnation and wherein it "rides time like riding a river."

Hopkins himself had sensed the reluctance of even the good pagan to accept what to the pagan mind would be the "limitations" of a Redemption effected in time, and he continues pensively in the same *Deutschland* stanza: "And here . . . the faithless fable and miss." The last clause of Hopkins' 1876 poem is a brilliant leap to the conclusion, documented some eighty years later by Eliade, that the myths of heathendom are efforts to escape the "dating" of history. To ask a pagan Greek *when* Prometheus stole fire from the gods would be to ask a senseless question: the mythical action is conceived of as outside real time. Because of its situation outside real time it commands reverence, and the priority which such an a-temporal event has over real human actions signals the worthlessness of temporal events. By the same token, to the pagan mentality the Incarnation, being in time, is a kind of religious farce. Mythological "events" are holy, while this historical event cannot be. We might combine Hopkins' insight and Eliade's findings in a Joycean pun: "the faithless, fabling, myths."

Yet even the faithful are not without weakness here, for they are not free of the heritage of pagan culture. The Catholic's immediate reaction to Hopkins' thought (as the present writer has had frequent occasion to observe in the case of those first confronted with Hopkins' poem) may be a kind of revulsion. Or at least the Catholic may prefer to leave this truth embedded indistinguishably in the mass of revelation which he accepts from the Church en bloc, rather than to have it baldly advertised. He may feel uneasy in its explicit presence. It seems not in keeping with God's dignity and importance and sanctity that His grace should be in a way channeled through the material universe. Yet this is precisely what happens when it comes to us through the Word made flesh, and only through the Word made flesh. The connection with the material universe is advertised even more by the doctrine of Mary's own special mediation in the economy of grace, for her role here is consequent upon her being Mother of God, consequent upon her furnishing out of her own body the material for the Incarnation.

Hopkins was aware, too, of this reluctance of his fellow Catholics, for his full line reads, "And here *the faithful waver*, the faithless fable and miss." Perhaps because of the residue of pagan culture which shows here and in which we all more or less necessarily live, even when we try to accept fully the implications of a religion embedded in history, our very notion of history is likely to be curiously circumscribed. In particular, when we think of the history of the Church herself, we are likely to think in what today is really a primitive frame of reference.

One instance of this is that studies of the relationship of the Church to the world, ancient or modern, are still all too likely to make their controlling frame of reference a politico-religious one rather than a larger, cosmological one. The politico-religious frame of reference is legitimate, of course, and if an individual author wishes to discuss the presence of the Church in the modern world in terms of the *Ancien Régime,* the French Revolution, Napoleon, the Kulturkampf in Germany, the loss of the temporal power of the Papacy, Mussolini, Hitler, and Communism, one can have no quarrel with him. He is speaking in terms which are convenient and familiar, even though it is not easy to relate all of them directly to the truths of revelation, either pro or con: revolution, monarchy, democracy, restorations, establishments, liberalism, *coups d'état,* independence, majority right, minority protests, and so on.

The somewhat curial approach to the place of the Church in history which the prominence of such terms in one's thinking indicates has much to recommend it. Indeed, the approach must be made familiar to those who wish really to put Christ's teachings into effect in the world around them, for God's purposes are not normally to be served by calculated ignorance, even of the political pressures which have annoyed religious purists (such as, for example, Roger Williams) but with which even purists must in the long run deal (sometimes, unfortunately, with a hypocrisy directly proportionate to their purism). As man in ancient times was already able to see, political activity is an important and praiseworthy human activity, and there is nothing necessarily despicable in it at all, although traffic in the City of Man always creates some mysterious tension in those devoted to the City of God.

A difficulty arises with this politico-religious analysis of the relationship between the Church and the world chiefly when, consciously or unconsciously, we tend to regard it as in itself somewhat adequate. I do not mean that we are likely to regard it as adequate on the supernatural level. After "explanations" of the relationship between the Church and the world cast in these curial terms are all in, Catholics instinctively feel that the history of the Church is not fully accounted for, since the story of the Church's work in the individual soul, the real story of God's grace, has not been told. The principal danger is not in imputing to the politico-religious treatment a false adequacy which would minimize the action of the Church on the individual (although there is some danger of this, too). Rather, the danger is that we may impute to it a false adequacy as it regards precisely the world and the relationship of the Church to the world, taking "the world" in its quite general meaning of that aspect of reality which is not genuinely and patently in itself religious—the secular, if we take this word in the sense which implies no active hostility toward religion. Does the politico-religious framework adequately define the relation of the Church to the secular universe? It appears not. For in the relationship between the Church and the secular universe something has occurred in modern times which has changed the very idea of a religio-political framework as this idea has been construed in the past.

In this thermonuclear, quasi-unified world where we now live, what, for instance, has happened to the classical notion of the sovereign state itself as an individuated institution competing with other sovereign states? The notion has not, of course, completely disappeared. We still live by it to some extent and shall continue to do so for some time. But we now know that the reality which this notion attempted to represent is doomed. The discrete and integral sovereign state or *respublica* is really not the sort of thing which Plato or Guicciardini or Hobbes or Jefferson thought it was, for it is not a stable item in human society. It is essentially an institution which comes into being at a certain stage in man's occupation of this planet and which subsequently begins imperceptibly to alter as mankind secures a better hold on itself and on the world by increase in population and advances in communication, with all that these things involve. Already "sphere of influence" has displaced the notion of sovereign state in many of the realities of political life.

Our notion of the state and of the political has undergone an enormous change in the past few generations because we have improved our knowledge of the relationship of man to the universe and of the relationship of both man and the universe to time and space. Once geology and astronomy and physics and anthropology have plunged the story of man into the depths of a universe between five and ten billion years old, still expanding with incredible speed through spaces measurable only by billions of light years, and once the history of literature, of philosophy, and of science has revealed the tremendous development which has gone on within the realm of human understanding vis-à-vis the reality with which man has found himself surrounded, we can hardly afford to think about the past without situating it somehow in our imaginations within this huge depth of time and space in which we now know we dwell.

Religiously, these time and space depths would perhaps have made little difference to an Aristotle, professing, as Aristotle did, that God is too exalted above all other reality to be in any way concerned with it (perhaps somewhat as Aristotle and his friends may have felt themselves to be exalted in the regard of the slaves of Athens). Even today, the same depths of time and space might not impress a yogi, intent on special arrangements for achieving direct union with the deity. But for a Christian the depth of vision brought by the new discoveries makes a tremendous difference, for he knows that no union with God is possible except through Christ, the Second Person of the Blessed Trinity, Himself God, Who deliberately took to Himself a human nature in this very world about which science is discovering so much. The follower of Christ is thus very much concerned with this physical world, and his thinking about the Church's place in it must keep pace with the natural knowledge we have about it.

As man's ideas of what the world is undergo radical revision and enlargement, the Christian must make some fundamental adjustments in thinking about his religion itself. But he must make them sensitively and within the economy of faith. The Modernists mistakenly tried to adjust revelation to the new facts, as though the new facts gave them some sort of new grasp on revelation. The obverse was what was called for, and it demanded more maturity and patience: not the adapting of revelation to the facts, but the integration of the new facts with revelation; not a new understanding of faith and of God in the light of the new discoveries, but a new understanding of the new discoveries in the light of faith and in relationship to God. What was called for by the new discoveries was not precisely a new understanding of Christ's divine Nature but a deeper and more adequate understanding than had hitherto been possible of His human nature (as well as of our own, which is the same essentially as His) brought about by the increasing knowledge concerning the relationship of man to the totality of the universe.

A new world view has come into being as man has moved from the age of Newtonian physics into the age of Planck,

Einstein, and Heisenberg, and, as Dr. Karl Stern has suggested, into the still newer (but strangely more familiar) world of depth psychology. My difficulty with the politico-religious frame of thinking as applied to the relationship between the Church and the modern world is that it operates without reference to the new world view. The frame of thinking becomes particularly limiting insofar as we are aware that the most significant and profound effect of the modern world on the Catholic Church has not been the loss of the Papal States or the running fight with anticlericalism or even with Communism, but precisely the slow, and sometimes exceedingly painful, elaboration of a more profound understanding of herself and of her role in God's designs forced by the changing world view.

For the Church has elaborated her understanding of her mission, and indeed come to some new understanding of this mission, insofar as the relationship of man to the universe has been clarified through the scientific work of the modern world. The Church is Christ's Mystical Body, inextricably involved with His human nature, and the development of our understanding of man inevitably makes itself felt in the Church's understanding of her own mission.

III

Basically, the reorientation which the modern world has demanded in man's understanding of the universe and of himself is a reorientation around the fact of evolution—cosmic, organic, and intellectual. This reorientation underlies the Church's activity even at the politico-religious level, and, although it does not explain everything in her relationship to the modern world, it adds a new dimension to almost all the elements in every explanation.

The modern preoccupation with revolution, not only as a political phenomenon or device but also as a philosophical theme and a way of life, is an epiphenomenon of this reorientation. The rigidity of the supporters of the *Ancien Régime* and of those who opposed the *Ralliement* announced by Cardinal Lavigerie at the instance of Leo XIII, as well as of those who were piqued at the "socialism" of *Rerum Novarum,* is connected with an inability to enter imaginatively into the fact of social evolution or even to recognize the fact. The failure of the Catholic mind rather generally throughout Europe to adjust promptly and adequately to the emigration from the farms to the factories and the attempt to meet social change by anachronistic talk about remaining content with one's "state in life," still conceived of in terms of a static universe, reflect the same inability.

On the other side of the ledger, the drive to social reform manifest in *Rerum Novarum* and elsewhere reflects the slow growth of the realization that human society is always an evolving thing. The "Americanist" quarrel presents the same problem of change in another epiphany, and the Modernist movement represents a particularly disastrous attempt to deal with this urgent problem in too simple a fashion, proceeding as though change alone, and not the more arduous dialectic of change and changelessness, might define the province of human activity and constitute the field for divine revelation.

To recognize the profound changes in man's view of the universe and of himself in it which has marked modern times does not mean that the politico-religious view must be scanted, for the developments which such a view discerns and details are themselves coefficients of the growth in man's understanding of the cosmos and his place in it. But to think of the Church as being "in" the modern world chiefly through her dealings with the great political powers is to minimize both the notion of the modern world and of the Church's presence, and at this point somewhat to obscure the relationship of Christ and of His Church to the cosmos as a whole.

To a certain extent the politico-religious framework is common today and must be used because of the nature of secondary-school and even elementary-school training, which in our civilization still tends to view history as primarily military and political—not so much as in the past, but still to a notable extent. The live core of history, that is, the history of the development of the human psyche in the framework of human society over the ages, the history of the development of man's ideas, has not commonly made itself real below the college level of teaching or even at times below the graduate level. Undoubtedly it will never be able to penetrate the all-important beginning years of instruction so thoroughly as political history, for battles, whether military or political or personal, remain eminently easy for a youngster to understand. He has been in them. A military and political reading is thus the most facile reading which history can be given. And this, no doubt, is why the first historians wrote history from a military and political point of view. This view is the first one available.

But this view is no longer sufficient. It is no longer feasible, if it ever was feasible, for history to concern itself only with the past. The past must be studied with attention to the future. Not that one goes to history to secure and bear away a neat bundle of "lessons" with which henceforth to plot one's own life. This view of history, a relic of Renaissance pedagogical developments, is too facile to be convincing. But one does, by now, go to the past to get a sense of the trajectory along which the entire human race on our globe is moving.

Here certain larger theorems assert themselves as having an unmistakable bearing on the future: Man's history is tied in with that of the cosmos which bore him: he appears at a certain point in its development, after a vast maturity is reached. Thereupon the story of mankind on our earth is in great part the story of the progressive colonization of the planet in its entirety, combined with the story of developing communications and skills. After an initial racial differentiation, or scatter of variants, reminiscent of the progressive differentiation in infrahuman evolution, a pattern of convergence sets in in the human world. Over the entire surface of the earth men establish greater and greater contact with one another, generating an awareness of all mankind as a unit—in a way, for example, in which the global aggregate of bears or of butterflies never establishes any sort of global awareness of itself. Today we are on the threshold of a new stage; the earth is beginning to fill up with mankind, while at the same time communications are being perfected in such a way as to make possible human cooperation on a scale simply inconceivable even five thousand years ago, much less a hundred thousand years ago. Within this network of communications are poised our technological skills. And the space age has in some sense begun.

Thus history, if seen in sufficiently large perspectives, gives us some idea of what the future will be like, although the idea is necessarily indeterminate in many details. It is within this world which the larger view of cosmic history reveals to us and which has ahead of it a future both projected from and different from its past that the Second Person of the Blessed Trinity became incarnate and established the Church as His Mystical Body, the extension of His Incarnation in time and space.

It may not be necessary to think about these larger perspectives always when we are considering the place of the Church in the modern world. But the time has come when, unless we think about them sometimes—and rather regularly, so that they form the habitual backdrop for our historical awarenesses—we are really distorting our understanding of reality. In an age when management consultants for commercial enterprises are becoming increasingly globe-conscious and metaphysical because of the very sweep with which they view even the small details of human activity, it is no longer possible to think of politico-religious history in the ways congenial to Gibbon or Macaulay or Newman. Even the semi-mystical approach of St. Augustine will not suffice, although the City of God and the City of Man are with us still. We know too much about the cosmos which he did not know.

Is not one of the difficulties of the Catholic mind and imagination at present a widespread inaptitude for viewing the Incarnation and Redemption against the full background of cosmic history as we know this history today? With this does there not go an unhealthy diffidence with regard to thinking honestly and constructively about the future—the full future, not the next five or ten or fifty years but the next thousand or hundred thousand years? It is perfectly true that neither you nor I can hope to set up a program for Catholic activity or for any other activity which is at all likely to be feasible ten or twenty thousand years from now. But it is also true that unless we habitually feel our activity and decisions to be somehow involved in the long-range future, just as we now know them to be involved with the far, far distant past, we can no longer make decisions which will be very real in the twentieth century present. Unless we have a sweeping view of history in its most profound reaches—psychological, sociological, intellectual, and cosmic, as well as religious and political—the Church will not be present in us to the modern world. For one of the most distinctive notes of the modern mind is its conscious and deliberate sweep into the past and the future in all their dimensions.

2
Religious-Secular Dialogue in a Pluralist Society

If we take a certain nineteenth century curial approach to the question of religious pluralism in modern society, it is virtually impossible to consider pluralism as anything other than a defection. For in this politico-religious approach is inherent the presumption that at some time in the past "everybody" was a member of a united religious as well as secular community. In its extreme form such an approach even implies that a supposedly otherworldly outlook was practically universal among men. From such a presumably unified, otherworldly religious state of affairs, we are to suppose that there has arisen somehow our present age of secular depravity, bearing religious pluralism as its fruit.

This point of view is becoming increasingly less inviting. As human society over the face of the globe develops toward greater unification, it becomes increasingly less convincing to base our notion of what "everybody" was or was not on impressions projected out of no more than a European past, and that a highly idealized one. Religious pluralism must be viewed not in terms of an essentially parochial history but, so far as possible, in terms of the total development of our earth and of the cosmos.

II

To consider any model from the past as the realization of the Christian ideal of unity is to belie this ideal itself. The romantic concept of medieval Europe, which is the model most often resorted to here, will not do at all. According to this concept, European society is taken as a self-sufficient and entirely integral unit threatened only by the incursions of the Mohammedans and Mongols and a few others, who supposedly always took the initiative in aggressiveness and thus made evident their own perversity, thereby also rendering forceless any questions which might arise concerning the real problems of conscience faced by a Christian vis-à-vis Islam. In this view Christians are envisioned as living in something called "Christendom," which is taken to be a self-sufficient unity not faced with any real problems outside its own perimeters and in adequate control of the problems within.

The fallacy in this view is that anyone outside the perimeters of Christianity is by that very fact a problem for Christians, since the Christian is a man with the Gospel, the Good News, which is destined for all men and which he is obliged to make known to those who have not heard of it. Thus, ideally a medieval Christianity possessed by ancient memories of the Nestorians in India and China, or later stirred by the voyages of Marco Polo or by the reports of the thirteenth- and fourteenth-century Franciscan and Dominican emissaries to the Mongols recently edited by Christopher Dawson, or even by the compilations circulated under the name of Sir John Mandeville, could by no means consider itself a self-contained unit. It was necessarily an incompleteness. However replete with Christianity Christendom might be up to its very boundaries, Christian society was in no real way a complete society until the Good News had been brought to all men.

Of course, it could be urged that effective preaching of the Gospel to lands as little known to Christians as China and India was impossible in the thirteenth and fourteenth centuries. But such a view is open to question. Carrying the Good News to such lands was physically and psychologically difficult, yes, but hardly impossible. Several embassies of Christians had reached the Grand Khan himself. And if such embassies could reach their destination, why might not sizable groups of missioners have attempted to bring the Good News to the Far East? Kublai Khan's request, reported by Marco Polo, to have a hundred learned Christians sent him to prove the truth of the Christian faith aroused little response in the West.

There was, one might urge, too much to do at home. But there always is. At the very time he was preaching the Gospel elsewhere, St. Paul was writing his letters to the Corinthians and the Philippians and the Colossians in an effort to straighten out the chaos he had had to leave behind. The fact is that medieval man's vision of the Catholicity of the Church here failed somehow to stir the medieval imagination religiously, even when the presence of Tartar slaves in Europe suggests that the imagination had been stirred to some extent commercially. It may not have been the fault of medieval man, but his vision of Catholicity did leave something to be desired.

The fact is that medieval society was supported not only by the minimal development of communications but also too often by a more or less conscious effort to shrink what communications there were. This enabled the medieval West European Christian to keep his imagination relatively clear of involvement with persons who were not Christians, as though they did not really concern him. Even granted that this state of mind is quite understandable because of the insecurity of life five or six hundred years ago, it was not in itself a desirable state of mind for a Christian. The state of mind belongs to the medieval age rather than to the Christian ethos. The ghetto was a typical medieval institution, we might recall, maintained by cooperation of medieval Christians with medieval Jews.

Despite the avowedly Catholic mission of the Church, premodern Christianity often fell too easily into the habit of thinking of Christendom and of religion generally in terms of geographical divisions and frontiers. Insofar as it did so, it really blinked the problem of coexistence, and indeed of pluralism. For a Christian especially, all mankind is one. If the medieval Christian had faced this fact squarely, he would have been aware that he was already living in a kind of pluralism. So was everyone, but the condition should have been even more evident to the Christian than to others.

There were certainly very real reasons for medieval man's attitude toward coexistence—or rather for his lack of a very positive attitude. The underdeveloped state of communications was one. The absence of a habit of thinking in quantitative terms was another. When we today think of the coexistence of thirteenth century Christendom and heathendom, we almost automatically think of so many millions of persons here and so many there. (In preparing this chapter, at one point I began a search for such figures. The use of exact figures proved irrelevant almost immediately, but not until after I had thought seriously of using them.) Earlier man had no effective way of measuring large quantities of men. The first steps in modern demography were taken only toward the end of the Renaissance era.

In the total absence not only of reliable statistics but even of any general inclination to think in terms of statistics, not only about mankind but about reality generally, men all over the earth until the past few hundred years could not effectively imagine the multitudes of men outside their own immediate ken. While knowledge of what lay outside Christendom existed, it was so vague and so scattered that we can truly say that Christian theologians did not neglect the problem of mankind outside Christendom so much as they simply failed to be struck by the problem.

But to note the real obstacles, psychological and physical, to contact with other human beings felt on the one side by Christendom and by the Judaism to which it is so mysteriously related, and on the other side by the non-Hebraic and non-Christian world, is only to note that human society had not progressed to the point where the fact of pluralism, at least on a global scale, could be assessed and its problems faced in a real way. In earlier human existence, that is to say for most of the time man has been on the earth, religious differences had rather definite geographical correlatives. Since national sovereignty is defined largely in geographic terms, nationalism and religion have been almost inextricably interwoven in a geographical framework. *Cuius regio, eius religio* was a principle enunciated by Cicero with slightly different wording as a commonplace in his age: *Sua cuique civitati religio est, nostra nobis (Pro Flacco* 2. 8)—"Each commonwealth has its own religion, and we have ours." The principle obtained from prehistoric times until very recent years practically everywhere—Jean Jacques Rousseau, Comte, and others comment on its success in the ancient world—and it still obtains in most regions of the world with greater or lesser rigor. The temporal perspectives must be kept in evidence here: a principle such as this which has apparently obtained for some four hundred thousand years (a reasonably firm figure for man's existence on the earth) is not going to be obliterated in a mere few hundred years without considerable difficulty.

When nowadays in most Western societies, and in a growing number of Eastern societies, religious differences have correlatives other than geographical and nationalistic, and the problem of coexistence and pluralism thereby moves into a new stage, we must not be surprised if it does not move as fast as some shortsighted persons might expect it to do. As societies interact more and more on one another with our improved communications, issues become exceedingly complex. The Catholic Church, for example, finds herself engaged today with all sorts of civilizations simultaneously, working in a great many different time coordinates, from new industrial and semi-industrial civilizations to very old, retarded civilizations such as those in Papua, or, what is more difficult, with civilizations, such as those in Italy and other parts of Europe or in parts of Latin America, which are a mingling of highly industrial elements and elements from centuries-old folkways.

Still, it is helpful to remember that the most retarded civilization of today is hardly more retarded than all civilizations have been for most of man's life on the planet, for most of some four hundred thousand years. Not only now but since the original breakthrough a few thousand years ago, civilization generally has been advancing at a pace which by any realistic historical standards has been surprisingly rapid.

What I have noted here so far involves no new discoveries. It is intended, however, to encourage a special awareness. We gain perspective by realizing that in the Christian economy especially, but not exclusively, the problem of coexistence and pluralism is basically an old human problem, not a recent one. It has been with man from the beginning. If it has not appeared urgent until very recent times because of the dispersion of the human race in relatively isolated groups over the surface of the earth, we should remember that this dispersion is not a normal or durable human condition. In his writings on evolution and the "human phenomenon" Père Pierre Teilhard de Chardin, S.J., has made much of the fact that, although the infrahuman evolutionary pattern is typically "bushy," fraying out into greater and greater differentiation, greater and greater separation and divergence, the pattern of evolution within the human sphere, which is ultimately the sphere dominated by mind, by intelligence, is, on the contrary, convergent. All cultures inevitably move toward mergers with all other cultures.

Immediately after his appearance, it is true, man spreads out over the face of the earth and develops minor divergences, the sort we note as racial and national differences today, physical and cultural. But once man has pretty well occupied the surface of the globe and developed the kind of thinking which enables him to realize his larger social potentialities, a complementary pattern of convergence sets in, a pattern which continuously accelerates its own development. Despite iron and bamboo curtains, and our own often blameworthy reluctance to share what we know with others (comparable to their blameworthy reluctance to share what they know with us), man is still more in contact with man today than at any other period in the history of our globe. The age of geographical races, as the distinguished racial anthropologist Carleton Coon has said, is *passé*. The former disseverance and divergence of the one human race, like human ignorance itself, was not a durable human condition. Man is made to unite humanity.

A corollary is that any society, past or present, insofar as it seals itself off from other human societies, is an inhuman society. It may have, or it may have had, reasons for doing so. But these reasons must, as soon as possible, be done away with. Man is made to deal with other men, not with only a certain group of men; and human society as a whole is cohesive. Because of this fact—not to mention the further fact that, at least for a Christian, all human beings must be the objects of a love and solicitude which presupposes and goes far beyond the natural demands of humanity—the medieval types and other primitive types of coexistence by isolation, with their consequent pluralisms based on geographical divisions, are no longer acceptable. At best they have been tolerable for want of something better. But they are not a permanent condition; rather, they are full of tensions, fuller, in the long run, than our conditions in pluralistic societies today. The very lack of effective communications which lent plausibility to isolationism was a temporary condition, destined to be liquidated because of the very nature of man.

III

The breakthrough in geographical frontiers which has moved the question of coexistence into a new stage and made urgent the problems of pluralistic society has been marked not only by cataclysmic developments in communications which are forcing us to rethink our whole notion of human existence on our planet but also by a concomitant tendency of the communications process to work its way into man's mind as a frame of reference for his thinking about the universe and all being as well as about thought itself.

A cardinal point in this development within the past century and a half has been Hegel and the importance which he gives to dialectic. The notion of dialectic was old when Hegel laid hold of it, but with him it becomes urgent. However, the connection of dialectic with communication and in particular with real dialogue, the speaking of man to man, does not mean much to Hegel, and he could neither forecast nor foresee the stress on dialogue itself which marks our day and which leads Jaspers to state that "communication is the path to truth in all its forms." Yet in looking back, we can see that the veering of interest from nature philosophies to a dialectical philosophy is a noteworthy manifestation of a shift toward Jaspers' outlook. Other developments in Hegel's day foreshadowed our present interest in communication: the spread of literacy and the imminent development of the telegraph and of the other instruments serving communication which followed the telegraph in such short order: the telephone, wireless, television, radar, and radio telescope, as well as the various forms of rapid transit, from the steam locomotive to the jet plane.

Whatever the interrelations of these phenomena, the age which has emerged and in which we live can reasonably be styled the communications age. At least, this is the American's way of looking at it. The European would be more inclined to view it as the age of dialogue. But the two come to much the same thing, although they register typical national differences in outlook. For, whether we call it the age of communication or of dialogue, ours is certainly the age which has become explicitly conscious of the importance of man's sharing his thoughts with others, the age in which millions of persons are set aside to expedite this sharing and in which the influence of this sharing, and its absolute necessity, are increasingly matters of prime interest to the philosopher and theologian, just as much as they are to the manufacturer and marketing expert.

Although geographical boundaries are of course still far from being annihilated, the simple expedient of sealing off the frontier can never again be serviceable in solving human problems to the extent to which it was in an earlier age. We must not lose sight of the fact that this is what the earlier sealing off of the frontier was—a means of solving problems of human relations. The economic and military and social ramifications of isolationist politics may be very real. But they are all mere fronts for the basic problem of isolationism: the problems of man's personal relations with his fellow man. Today we have reached a point where we can realize more clearly that geographical isolation settles nothing, for it is inevitably a temporary measure, doomed by the very nature of man and of human society. The experiment which resulted in the foundation of Liberia in 1822 is unthinkable in 1959: white and Negro Americans are going to have to talk the situation out and improve their personal relations right here.

The earlier attempts to resolve essentially human problems by geographical manipulation are connected with a reliance on diagrammatic analysis of essentially human problems which no longer seems real to thinking men. No spatial framework, however elaborate, can deal adequately with the relationship of person to person which is the ground of all human activity. When we seek something in the sensorium in terms of which we can deal with person-to-person relationships, we find that we must deal with them also in terms of voice and speech and, ultimately, of sound.

The relationship between church and state or between the religious and the secular can profitably be studied in terms of dialogue, of voice, of speech between man and man. This is not quite the same as to view matters in terms of dialectic, Hegelian or other. Dialectic is, indeed, related to dialogue, for it is from dialogue between persons that the notion of dialectic is in one way or another derived. Nevertheless, dialectic is often given in philosophical discussion a formalistic, diagrammatic cast which we wish to avoid here. The three stages ordinarily associated with the Hegelian dialectic exhibit this diagrammatic or spatialized frame of mind: thesis (a "putting"), antithesis (a "putting against"), and synthesis (a "putting together"). I wish to cut back of such formalisms to the reality of a discussion or dialogue which establishes and develops relations between persons and to regard the church-state relationship and the religious-secular relationship by analogy with a discussion between persons.

New Testament prescriptions concerning the relationships between church and state or religion and secular culture have little of the spatial or diagrammatic about them. There is nothing like the prescription purported to be enshrined in the long Indian name for the Connecticut lake which means "You-fish-on-your-side-I-fish-on-my-side-nobody-fish-in-the-middle." There is nothing said of "territory" or "areas" of sovereignty. But there is reference to persons. Thus Jesus replies to his questioners, "Render to Caesar the things that are Caesar's, and to God the things that are God's" (Matthew xxii 21). Here is the state personalized in Caesar and contrasted with a personal God. To Pilate, Jesus says, "I am a king," but "My kingdom is not of this world" (John xviii 36–37). Here the Kingdom is His own personal rule. In a similar way Paul's familiar dialectical relationships, those between Jew and gentile (or Jew and Greek), converted gentile and unconverted Jew, converted Jew and unconverted gentile (Romans xi 7–23), bond servant and freeman, male and female (Galatians iii 28), are all presented basically not as relationships between abstract ideas but as dialogic relationships between persons. The same type of relationship governs St. Augustine's City of God and City of Man, or St. Ignatius Loyola's Standard of Christ and Standard of Lucifer; these, too, are relationships based on person-to-person oppositions.

This personal quality of dialogue is the first of the qualities relevant to the notion as it affects our present subject. The relationship of church and state to each other, or of the religious and secular to each other shows its personalist roots in various ways. For one thing, it is the relationship of two things not entirely manageable in terms of abstract ideas. It did not originate in abstraction and it cannot end there.

In its present form, the church-state tension came into being in the Roman Empire, when men personally committed to a personal God (in the tradition which the Christians shared with the Hebrews) stated, "We may not and will not worship the Roman gods, although we will be loyal to the Roman rule, and that because of the demands of the same faith which keeps us from worshiping the Roman gods." This stand jolted pagan society, which had presumed that one changed his religious stand according to political necessity, as one changed his civil position. But Christians were ready to die rather than change, as Hebrews had been before them, although the theocratic nature of Hebrew civil society seemingly precluded the loyalty to a pagan state which the Christians, following Pauline teaching (Ephesians vi 5), felt obligatory.

It was this stand which precipitated, and still precipitates, disputations about the tensions between church and state. The disputations did not precipitate the stand, but vice versa. The given, concrete Christian stand precipitated abstract theories about the separation of church and state.

The church-state tension is personal also in the sense that it is lived within the souls of individual persons. It is a tension which calls for constant individual action and decision on the part of those religiously committed. For the tension is one which can never be liquidated by formulas but is one to be lived through and to be lived with. This is not to say that formulas are irrelevant or unserviceable or untrue —to say this would be to belie the full tension of the situation. They are, or can be, very relevant and serviceable and true, but they are never complete when brought to bear on a concrete situation, where decision must always take into account matters which are unformulated.

Further, the church-state tension is personal because of the communal nature of the church. In *Man's Western Quest*,

Denis de Rougemont has pointed out the difference between the Jewish and Christian sense of communal worship and the worship in isolation found in other religions. The Christian notion of the church is adumbrated by the Hebrew notion of the people of God. Various Christians feel the communal notion of the church variously, but they all feel it to some degree. In the Catholic Church it is so strong that the central act of worship, the sacrifice of the Mass, is always and inevitably an act of the entire Church, even though the faithful may not be in attendance. (It is to be noted that it is forbidden for a priest, without special authorization, to celebrate Mass with no one else in attendance.) Indeed, since all Catholics' prayers are referable to this Great Prayer, there is a sense in which no Catholic's prayer can be entirely private. His prayer is always with the community.

If its personal cast is the first dialogic quality of the church-state, religious-secular relationship, a second, and related quality is its sense of direction combined with a lack of conclusiveness. Dialogue itself as such has purpose, but it has no particular terminus. Since the resources of personal give-and-take on which it draws are bottomless, a dialogue can always proceed further. Not only that, but it should proceed further if the lives of persons are to continue. This does not mean that it is incessant, but that, while it may be quiescent at any given moment, it is always alive and capable of further growth. Because the dialogue between church and state or between the religious and the secular is—in an analogous way, of course, but really—like the dialogue between persons, it cannot possibly be frozen off or entirely repressed. Persons may be distinguishable one from the other, but they prove their very distinctness by contact with those who are not themselves.

The Church herself needs to be *in* the world just as des-

Religious-Secular Dialogue in a Pluralist Society

perately as she needs not to be *of* it. And the state cannot with impunity pretend that religion, or anything else which exists, is non-existent.

The personal and inconclusive quality of the religious-secular relationship when thought of as a dialogue makes it a particularly painful reality to persons of a certain cast of mind which we might style visualist. If the City of God is related to the City of Man dialogically, we shall have to face the fact honestly that the two Cities cannot be thought of as related to each other by means of any neat spatial model.

We cannot in any satisfactory way imagine the state as existing on one side of a kind of lot and the church or churches on another side, with or without a wall of separation between them. To do so is to fall into a trap especially designed for himself and others by the sixteenth century savant Peter Ramus. Anxious to distinguish the various "arts" from one another and particularly rhetoric from logic, Ramus had recourse to this sort of suburban development-scheming in things of the mind. From the legislation of Greek antiquity he dredged up what he called "Solon's Law," which had prescribed in ancient Athens that alongside each wall be left a clear space of one foot, alongside each house a clear space of two feet, and so on. With the "constant undaunted resolution of maintaining his own Opinions" which Hobbes was later to share, Ramus persuaded himself and thousands upon thousands of followers that somehow or other there was an exact correspondence between the real estate situation in ancient Athens and the condition of logic and rhetoric in sixteenth century Europe. Rhetoric and logic—and indeed all the arts—were to be kept clear of one another in teaching by at least a foot or two all the way around. Unfortunately for Ramus, knowledge does not really exist in "zones," so that it became difficult, if not impossible, to know what his buffer zone of a foot or two around logic or rhetoric could in fact possibly mean.

Even so, Ramus seemingly had more confidence in human nature than some recent legists have had. He was content with a vacated buffer zone, an intellectual no-man's-land of very scant depth, to separate the areas of knowledge as he envisioned them. More recently, resorting to the same diagrammatic approach to church-state relationships, and under the influence of the visualist eighteenth century thinking retailed to us by Thomas Jefferson, but suspicious of mere empty space, we have sought to erect a "wall of separation" on the border between religious and secular culture.

But, whatever honest progress we may have made in our thinking, the wall has not helped much. For there is no satisfactory way of conceiving the reality of the church (or of religious activity) and the reality of the state (or of secular activity) as occupying two different plots of ground. "Good fences make good neighbors," Robert Frost reminds us. But how to consider religious activity and secular activity even as next-door neighbors when both are my own? The concepts are not related to each other in a very effective next-door way. When we are considering the religious-secular situation in terms of dialogue, we are considering it in a way which cannot be reduced to such visual models, no matter how elaborate such models may be made.

Its resistance to visualist formulation, which is to say "clear" formulation, is a third quality of the religious-secular situation. It is not simply that the dialogic situation is a moving one rather than a static one—although this is of some relevance, for the visualist mind is impatient until it has reduced all to quiescence, at least in the sense in which actual movement can be made static by being committed to an immobile drawing or chart or set of figures. The dialogic situation is more than moving. It is moving in a way which does not yield to diagramming, which cannot be adequately pictured or reduced entirely to "form."

The reason for this is that the movement of dialogue—and the religious-secular relationship insofar as it is like this movement—is essentially a movement concerned with an "I" and a "thou," and not with "objects." And there is no way for me to picture the intimate and incommunicable sense of self which makes known to me this "I" which I am, and no way to picture the correlative intimate and incommunicable self which I sense is you (or "thou"). I can express this self of mine by the mental and the spoken word "I" only by reason of the fact that I myself utter the word "I"—for this word means something decidedly different to me from what it does to you or to anyone else who uses it. And I can express your self by "you" or "thou" only by addressing myself *to* you. For, since "you" or "thou" means something quite different to every single one of the thousands of persons to whom I may speak it, it can be given definition and individual application within a real dialogue and only within a real dialogue. "You" means the person to whom I am actually addressing myself and for whom, *while I address him,* I can use no name, no *nomen,* no noun, but only this curious thing which we designate as a *pro-nomen* or pronoun, a substitute name. Unlike a real noun or name, the pronoun "thou" must be assigned its role, its reference, in terms of a going dialogue and in no other way. It signifies in terms of a personal sharing in every instance unique because it is between two unique persons. Of such a sharing I can form no picture and certainly no adequate diagram.

This "I" and "thou" are of course known in a situation which itself engages the object world, for although "I" and "thou" are not objects but persons, they are known to one another through dealings in terms of objects. I become aware of myself and of you as I talk *to* you *about* things. But by the same token, objects themselves are known to us in a dialogic situation, as we talk to another, or listen to another talking, about them.

Dialogue is thus moving, and lends motion to other things, not in the sense that it makes certainty about objects impossible, for it leads to many objective certainties (although not to certainty in everything), but in the sense that it is open to the continued and limitless influence of one person on another. Through dialogue, one person does not seek to annihilate another (although Sartre, in his calculating, one-sided exposition of half of the story, would try to have it this way, and perhaps Hegel's dialectic of master and slave would, too), nor even to understand another in the sense in which one understands an object, by "grasping" it. There is no way for one person to "grasp" another as he might "grasp" a mathematical theorem or a principle of economics. The "hold" which one person has on another is better called "appeal," which is to say a kind of "calling" (*appellare* means "to call"), and such appeal comes into being through love. By dialogue a person seeks not to grasp but to commune, to open himself to another and to enter into the other who has reciprocally opened his mind and heart to him.

For human beings, dialogue is thus developmental. It develops the persons who take part in it, enabling them to realize to a greater extent their own promise and perfections. Indeed, from one point of view the whole of human life is simply a dialogue with other men and with God. In the quality of the dialogue to which it has contributed, the measure of each human life can be taken.

IV

Because the church-state or religious-secular relationship thus ultimately resists complete and total formulation does not mean that it is unintelligible or that it cannot be dealt with. We must attempt all the limited formulations which are true and possible. But while we realize their truth, we must also realize their limitations, acknowledging that the problems here are not grounded in the relationship of object to object, of thing to thing, but in the commitment of person to person.

To think of religious-secular relationships in a dialogic rather than a diagrammatic fashion is thus to acknowledge their connections with the human person, for dialogue serves the needs of the human person. Here it will be helpful to consider some of the ways in which the church and the state, or the religious and the secular, affect the world of human persons as such.

In the West at least, the state has certainly in the course of history progressed more and more toward respect for the individual person. The ancient Greek or Roman state, supported directly on slavery, is superseded by the medieval European state in which, although some slavery certainly existed, most slavery had been mitigated to serfdom, and the so-called servile arts by which most persons subsisted were accorded a respect unknown among most peoples in ancient times. Such a society is succeeded by a somewhat piratical age of enlightened free enterprise in which, if millions of persons are repressed, a tremendous resentment builds up throughout society against their repression until we arrive at the social legislation which is a commonplace in our day. Conditions today are far from perfect, and yet this over-all pattern of development is certainly one which acknowledges the responsibility of secular society as a whole and, where necessary, of the state itself to make possible the personal development of each and every individual.

At the same time, however, that this respect for the individual human person is in many ways building up, the state itself is increasingly depersonalized. Part of this growth in depersonalization comes from mere growth in size. Personal contact between those in Washington and 170,000,000 individual citizens over the United States is less feasible than it was between the leader of an Anglo-Saxon *comitatus* and his small group of followers.

But there seems to be a necessary movement toward depersonalization in the evolution of government. Growth in size itself is not an accident, but necessary and intrinsic to the pattern of the evolution of human society as man fulfills his role of taking over the earth. Moreover, the very notion of justice to which the state is committed has something impersonal about it. For the personal God of Jews and Christians, His mercy, not His justice, is above all His works. But in a secular society no one can be found who has a personal relationship to all members of society even remotely as intimate as that of a personal God. As a consequence, the personal claims of any man to rulership of secular society are, in the last analysis, extremely weak. It is not too surprising that, as society in the West becomes more elaborately organized, the symbols of personalism are in many ways sloughed off. Most notably, the king himself, who concentrates secular authority in a rule to which he succeeds by birth and which cannot be alienated from his person, fades away as an effective part of the secular order, and with him his satellite nobility.

It is false, of course, to assume that the state is ever completely depersonalized. As Martin Buber has pointed out, even the most complexly bureaucratic structures of contemporary society are still made up of persons and of personal decisions. Nevertheless, the time arrives when it is no longer possible to equate the state in the West with a person. *L'état c'est moi* becomes an anachronism.

What happens in the state happens in a parallel fashion in secular life generally, as the smaller, personalized units of activity are absorbed—never entirely, but to a great extent—in the larger, more systematized units which mark our age. As organization moves in, the personal to some extent suffers. For, as Buber again has pointed out, the "I" and the "thou" cannot be organized; only the "it" can be.

And yet, since it is persons who in the last analysis effect organization, it is not surprising that under these conditions men immediately devise compensations for the depersonalizing momentum which organization can develop, and devise the compensations *within* organization itself. At one level, and a low one, there is the "personal touch," the gift which is made by a machine and then "personalized" by having something added to it which had been made by another machine, but which somehow allows one's good intentions to show. At a slightly higher level, there are the personnel director, the personnel consultant, and the counselors who haunt the peripheries of our lives. At a still higher level, men in our day have worked out a personalist philosophy, a philosophy of the "I" and the "thou," thereby making the age which in one way has depersonalized itself into the age more conscious of the human person than any age before. I do not mean that everywhere today the human person is honored more than before: but in the over-all pattern of human society, I believe the person is.

Three things should be noted in connection with the emergence of a militantly personalist philosophy. First, this philosophy did not emerge until there were a large number of persons on earth—the very antithesis of mass and person helped make evident the sacredness and uniqueness of the person as never before. In earlier ages, men had found comfort in vaunting their minds or their powers of speech over the powers of nature, thereby assuring themselves of their own excellence. Because this entailed such intense concentration upon things, there was little time or effort or interest left over to assure the human individual of his own importance. He was left to assume this importance—often against terrible odds, in the face of facts which controverted it on every hand. With the evidence of man's mastery over vast areas of nature (not by any means all areas) he has had time to think through his own value, as well as his dependence, vis-à-vis his fellow man—his dependence, for sociology, too, is a product of the modern age (if not so recent a one as a personalist philosophy).

This brings us to the second point, namely, that the personalist outlook is dependent upon a high degree of organization in human society—organization of the "it," if you will, but organization which it is not wise to belittle or scorn. Of course, a personalist philosophy is itself a kind of organization and as such is not the same as what we might call a "going" "I"—"thou" relationship, but I believe no one would maintain that it has nothing to do with such a relationship.

The third thing to note in connection with the emergence of a militantly personalist philosophy is this: even though it may be considered with other philosophies as in certain ways a secular enterprise, such a philosophy tends to develop almost immediately religious overtones. Aristotelian nature philosophy can be concerned with God, but it is with a kind of thing-God who, as Aristotle with some plausibility maintained, was quite unconcerned with the doings of anything below Himself. This approach to the divine is a kind of polar opposite to real religious practice. A personalist philosophy, whether in Kierkegaard, Gabriel Marcel, or Dr. Buber is not so distant from religious reality. It turns on personal commitment.

V

It thus appears that social organization has generated as one of the correctives for its own depersonalizing tendencies certain movements which rise toward the religious. We can next turn to the question of religion itself, asking how personal the sphere of religion and of the church is as compared with that of the state. I shall here center my attention on the Catholic Church and the Catholic religion for the reason that I can speak from the fullest acquaintanceship and experience here, although I shall try not to exclude other religions or religious views, bringing these in where I can, at least by inference, and allowing the reader to fill in or correct my remarks out of his own knowledge and experience.

By every test it would seem that in the dialogue between the secular and the religious, it is the latter which speaks with the more personal voice, at least within the Hebraeo-Christian tradition. In a remarkable chapter in his remarkable book *Mimesis,* the late Erich Auerbach makes a point about the difference between the literature of the Greeks and the Old Testament by adverting to the opening of the twenty-second chapter of Genesis: "And it came to pass after these things that God did tempt Abraham, and said to him, Abraham! and he said, here I am." Nowhere in Greek literature, explains Auerbach, can such a passage be matched. Homer portrays his heroes rather exhaustively, so that the reader has virtually no questions to ask about their personal histories when Homer is finished. But the Biblical characters, both God and Abraham, burst onto the scene as persons thrust themselves into our lives, immediate but also mysterious, for, as real persons, they act from motives which are not entirely clear to the onlooker and which lead us back into the mysterious depths of the individual personality with its own individual and bottomless history.

This personal setting for the contact between God and man is essential to the Hebraic and to the Christian tradition, and without it the Bible, Old Testament and New Testament, is quite meaningless. This personal contact exists under all organization or "structure" in Hebraic and Christian tradition, and gives organization or structure its necessity and its meaning and its role.

When we look in the Hebrew and Christian tradition for what distinguishes the sacred from the secular, we find that the sacred is somehow governed by the individual conscience vis-à-vis its God. Here is the realm of real love and of real sin—not of feelings of guilt which the psychiatrist must handle, but of defection from what should be the object of personal love. A conscience which is formed solely on abstract principles, if such a conscience is possible, without reference to a personal God is, from a Christian point of view, a secular conscience.

The Catholic is of course committed to his religious position by reason of his conscience: defection from it would be for him defection from a personal commitment and obligation to a personal God. His attitude toward the visible Church is governed by this interior commitment. For this Church is not a mere "organization" but a mysterious extension of the Person of Christ, Who is Himself God. It is the Mystical Body of Christ.

Because of the interiority of the human person which she acknowledges and respects, the Catholic Church in her own laws makes explicit allowance for a division which the civil law does not know: that between the external forum, which concerns the law as it is a basis for the Church's public judgments, and the internal forum, which concerns the law as it relates to a person's own interior conscience. A person who has violated a law publicly in the external forum and incurs some sort of censure for this violation may, in the internal forum, be in quite good standing.

For example, to be excommunicated a Catholic must have done something wrong which is morally imputable to him—an excommunication cannot be attached to any other kind of action. Let us take a case in which an act to which an excommunication is attached—for example, a man's entering that section of the convent of nuns which is "cloistered," that is, which is set aside as the living quarters of the nuns and from which he is excluded—and suppose that such an act is performed out of inadvertence or simple ignorance of the law. Since no real sin is committed, no excommunication is incurred. Although in the external forum his excommunication would be presumed by those who knew of the external act, he would not really have been excommunicated in the internal forum, which is to say, as far as his conscience goes. Ordinarily the internal forum and the external forum correspond, but when they do not, it is the *internal* which the Church herself in her *externally* promulgated laws explicitly recognizes as the more important.

For this reason, that is, the Church's persistent concern with the individual's conscience above all externalities, the external organization of the Catholic Church appears in constant danger of crumbling. The "it" of her laws is always yielding to the "I"–"thou" relationship of their application. Where the Church most closely touches the individual conscience, in the confessional, the relationship is strictly man-to-man, so much so that the Church can demand to know nothing whatsoever about the state of the individual conscience there revealed, or about the action which her minister, the priest, has taken with regard to it.

The priest himself is obliged in conscience to follow God's law and the Church's law—in itself impersonal, for its function is to make it impossible for one man to dominate over another simply as a person. Yet his application of the law is made in a real dialogic situation between persons which is inviolate.

The confessor is the public minister of the Church and of God's pardon, but his public role is so private that—short of the penitent's special permission to do so—he can never say anything to anyone else, in the Church or out, which would reveal the failings which the penitent has disclosed to him. At this focal point of the public administration of the Church, what is public and external, and controlled by public and external laws, is swallowed up in privacy, a privacy which is constituted by a judicial dialogue. Nothing quite like this is thinkable in secular law because of the less personal setting of the secular.

The intimacy which governs even the external ministrations of the Church and gives them their highly personal cast makes it understandable why the principal treatment of the Church in the writings of St. Thomas Aquinas occurs not in the *Summa theologiae,* but in his *Explanation of the Canticle of Canticles.* This intimacy and love are at the root of the Church's being, but, as the body is very much in evidence in the Canticles, so the Church has her body, too. Indeed, the Church is, in Catholic teaching, not simply an organization but a mysterious extension of the Person of Christ Himself: the Church is His "Mystical Body," involving the persons within her fold in His personal destiny in history.

It is not without good reason that in his book mentioned above, *Man's Western Quest,* Denis de Rougemont, convinced that man's Western quest has been the appreciation of the value of the human person, has traced the urgent concern with the person in the West back to the first three ecumenical councils of Nice, Constantinople, and Ephesus. Here, where the Church as an organism is battling through the capital questions of the consubstantiality of the Father and the Son, the divinity of the Holy Spirit, and the unity of the Person in Christ, we find the seeds of this concern with the person which has grown ever since. It would be untrue to say that all concern with person traces to a source in revelation. The term *persona* arose in Greek secular culture and was taken over by Christians. But within the Christian economy the notion has received its plenary development. Even Dr. Buber's personalism is by no means a purely Jewish development. It is the product of a fine Jewish mind operating under strong Christian influences.

The foregoing instances serve merely as samples of the personalism one finds rooted in religion in the Hebraic and Christian tradition, even where this tradition manifests most clearly its organizational aspects. In this connection, too, we should not fail to note one important fact: although a person is precisely that utter interiority and simplicity to which the concept of "organization" can hardly be applied, it is nevertheless the so-called "organized" religions which have kept most alive the sense of a personal God. When in the Jewish and Christian tradition strict religious "organization" has been depreciated in favor of purely personal religion or loosely held-together ethical societies, by an apparently inescapable momentum God begins to be assimilated to some impersonal "force." There may be some exceptions to this theorem, but the over-all pattern is unmistakable.

VI

The strangely personalizing function of strictly religious organization in the Hebraic and Christian tradition is highly important, for it shows that organization in the church and organization in the state are in reality quite different things. The concept of "power" associated with "organization" and "institutionalization" is at best a very difficult concept to use in a meaningful way with regard to human society and activity. To use the concept indiscriminately for religious organization and for secular organization, conceiving of these as opposed to each other in the way in which two taps on a common source of energy might be, is to dissociate oneself from actuality and to retreat into the unresolved conflicts of one's own subconscious.

As we have seen, the organization of the state moves away from a stress on a central or governing person to a kind of impersonality. It cannot avoid doing this, for its organization is concerned precisely with what is exterior about man: at least in the American tradition the state carefully dissociates itself from the personal life and choices of the individual so far as it can. It can never do so entirely, but it can come close to approximating a neutrality here.

Here the problem of commitment of the individual to the state arises. Loyalty or commitment has a high personal charge. It demands a personal setting in which to grow and become real. To what can loyalty or commitment be directed in the case of a depersonalized state?

It is common to maintain that persons are loyal to an "idea" or to an "ideal." But really to determine such an ideal, to give it definition, to formulate it, to assign it content is often not an easy thing to do. Some recent political studies have shown—as though we were not aware already—how often voting is influenced not by the ideals professed by one or another political party but by the symbolic appeal of the persons for or against whom one votes.

The difficulty of formulating the notion of democracy in a way satisfactory to all who profess devotion to it is well known. This difficulty is not peculiar to democracy. Communism, which professes to be a more complete, and indeed an exhaustive, political ideology, exercises its real large-scale appeal through the persons of leaders who are accorded a secular form of canonization suggesting the politico-religious canonization of the emperors of ancient Rome.

Throughout the political order we note this tendency to substitute for ideals, which are supposed to furnish operative goals, persons, who really make possible the personal commitment of others. For persons need no determination or definition or formulation. They are there, given realities—mysterious and impenetrable, but for all that the most real things we know. It is their reality which makes our commitment possible. For commitment is a form of love, and what we must love in the last analysis is not ideas or ideals but a person, a "thou" which provides the resonance which our person requires.

I do not call attention to the depersonalizing momentum in the modern state because of any belief that such a momentum is not good. It would seem that it is good, and that it is normal for a state, while learning to respect more and more individual human persons, to become itself more and more impersonal in its administrative aspects. I do not at all believe that a regression toward feudalism or other systems of personalized, and somewhat whimsical, administration would be desirable. But there is a danger in the case of the modern state, a danger of self-deception on the part of the citizenry. Since the state as such is in great part depersonalized, and since our own drives and personal commitments, when they are most urgent and most effective, are inextricably involved in persons, we can deceive ourselves into thinking that our commitments and actions stand on grounds more abstract than is the case. More often they are to groups of real persons, invested perhaps with more or less symbolic reference to other persons outside our immediate purview. We need to be aware of the personal ground of many of our supposedly impersonal secular commitments, and to the fact that our loyalty in a democracy is, in some way or other, actually a commitment to all of the millions of persons who make up our democratic society much more than it is loyalty to any "principles."

VII

In handling the problem of church-state or religious-secular relationships today in American society, it would seem that we should pay more attention to personal relationships, of which in many ways democratic society is becoming increasingly conscious. Society is a curious whole of which the parts—human persons—are also wholes. A democracy is a society which respects the wholeness of the persons of which it is composed and which derives its special strength from their wholeness. It is a society thus destined to live in a constant state of tension.

There is thus a sense in which democracy encourages love, for commitment is a form of love. This is not to say, however, that democracy is evangelical, that it performs the same role as religion, that it belongs to the City of God. It is only to say that what develops in a democracy can serve the purposes of the City of God. God's Kingdom is one of grace, and supernatural charity is more than the civil love which a citizen has for all his fellow citizens. Yet this love is more congenial to God's Kingdom than hate would be.

Dialogue has been our focus here because it is a way of achieving unity while preserving difference—the basic difference between one person and another. But it can also command our attention as a therapeutic.

In this world persons do live under the constant threat of war, not only between nations but between individuals themselves. Institutions, such as democracies, which encourage persons to develop themselves become involved in this same threat. A democracy may perish in the cataclysm when its citizens come to blows. In the face of this threat dialogue within a democracy does not guarantee peace, but it promotes it.

Dialogue is an action whereby an individual asserts—and even in the first instance discovers—his own uniqueness by the very process of uniting himself with another or others. The prelude to war is to halt dialogue, to cease to talk, to break off diplomatic relations. So long as groups in a pluralist society continue talking to one another, they cannot be entirely hostile. Our dialogue should, moreover, look not only or chiefly to establishing points of disagreement, although it may have to do this. It must find points of agreement, too.

All communication, all dialogue, has this effect: it unites, and this despite the greatest difference there is, that between your person and mine, between you and me. But, finally, dialogue must be between persons who are fully persons by being committed, by having taken a stand in the world of persons. Otherwise it will degenerate into the mere talk of a television commercial. In the tension between personal commitment and a love, not for humanity but for all individual men, the promise of a free society will best be realized.

3
Father Hecker
and the American Situation

Considered even from a natural point of view, the symbolism in which a person conceives and expresses his ideals is highly significant, and generally more significant than he himself is aware. In the important and critical statements he makes, a man inevitably says more than he means—or, from the converse point of view, means more than he explicitly says.

This fact is utilized by psychiatrists to help a person find the conflicts which he has hidden from himself and which, beneath the symbols, gnaw at his peace of soul. The man whose conversation comes around again and again to "the boss"—whether he wants to be just like the boss or hates the boss thoroughly—reveals by this very fixation on a figure symbolizing authority a great deal about himself, his own ambitions and emotional needs. The child who identifies himself with a cowboy, not only in a passing game but passionately throughout the day, is trying desperately to organize his emotions and ambitions around a symbol of manliness, however ineffectual. The insane frequently identify themselves with some symbol of absolute power—Napoleon is the classic favorite here—so as to be able to impose their unreal view of life on the world around them by a simple *fiat*.

If our use of natural symbolism manifests the hidden wellsprings of our motivations and drives, will not our use of the symbols involved in divine revelation manifest our hidden life even more? Revelation is not only historical; it is highly symbolic. How could it be otherwise when it terminates in the manifestation of the Word, Who is the very expression, the Symbol of the Father? The symbols used by God in divine revelation have a natural base—water, washing, the natural spoken word—but they are also involved in the dense reality of history which is centered on the Incarnate Word of God. For God's revelation comes to man only in time and in history. Thus, in Hebrew and Christian revelation symbols come not only psychologically charged but historically charged as well. For, as St. Thomas Aquinas and others have pointed out, man makes words signify truth, but God, the Master of history, makes persons and things in connection with Christ signify truth by making real historical persons and things and events mean something more than just themselves. Thus Moses somehow really *signifies* Christ. Israel really signifies the Church. And the children of Rachel referred to in Jeremias signify in some mysterious way the Holy Innocents, as the Gospel according to St. Matthew makes quite clear.

II

Isaac Thomas Hecker was by nature sensitive to the symbolic around him, and he had been further sensitized by his early religious upbringing and by his intimacy with the Transcendentalists even before he entered the Catholic Church as a young man of twenty-five. His sensitivity to symbols grew within the Church. It was a sensitivity which ranged beyond religious symbols out into the secular world. Hecker was particularly sensitive to America as a symbol, and to certain symbols by which Americans lived—liberty, the ideal of hard work, expansiveness and "optimism," resourcefulness—and he was burning with a desire to infuse these ideals with a Catholic spirit. Little wonder that he himself in his own day became, and still remains, a symbol of the Church in America.

When Father Hecker and his companion priests, Fathers Augustine F. Hewit, George Deshon, and Francis A. Baker, set about founding a society of priests to bring the Catholic Church into more intimate relationship with American life and to win non-Catholic Americans to the Church, they felt themselves moved to call the society after the Apostle Paul—the Missionary Society of St. Paul the Apostle, whose members, through their more than one hundred years of devoted work for the Church, have been known affectionately everywhere as Paulists. True to their Catholic instincts, these men reached back into history to find a symbol for their dedication of themselves to Christ.

What special symbolic value could St. Paul have had to the early Paulists to bring them to call themselves after him? He is a symbol of, among other things, missionary zeal, and the term "Missionary" in the name of the Paulist group indicates that this was an aspect of Paul's character and career which appealed. But we have here no full explanation. There were many other missionaries besides St. Paul. Why single him out? A reason can be found in the peculiar cast of his missionary work: he was the Apostle of the Gentiles. And, although Paulists were not exactly going to the Gentiles, but rather, for the most part, to baptized Protestants, it appears that the title Apostle of the Gentiles is highly relevant here. It suggests a more profound reason why Paul appealed to the Paulists, and a reason why his situation was and is a curiously relevant one for the United States. For, a Jew sent to the Gentiles, Paul of Tarsus was certainly a man between two worlds. He was this in a variety of ways.

It is a profoundly Christian situation, to be caught between two worlds. Of course, all men, Christian or not, are caught between two worlds at least in the sense that they are made up of body—with its matter billions of years old— and of soul, which for each man in an instant leaped into existence from God's hand by special creation, unique and unduplicable. But Christians have the tension between two further worlds to feel and live with. Christians are, both body and soul, citizens of this temporal world and citizens of the Kingdom of God. They have responsibilities to both these realms.

Paul, too, knew the two worlds of matter and spirit, for he, too, was made up of body and soul. He, too, as a Christian felt the double allegiance which both his body and soul owed to the temporal order and to the Kingdom of his Master. He was a citizen of Tarsus in Cilicia, he reminds the Roman tribune (Acts xxi 39), taking care to point out to the tribune that his native Tarsus was "no mean city." Moreover, as he reminds the tribune again, he was a Roman citizen, with the rights and duties attaching to this status, and he was a Roman citizen not merely by naturalization but by birth (Acts xxii 25). Like his Master, Paul teaches that a man has a serious obligation to be a responsible member of the human community of this world, to render to Caesar what is Caesar's, and that this obligation binds not only man's body but his soul, his interior attitudes as well, "not serving to the eye, as it were pleasing men, but, as the servants of Christ doing the will of God from the heart" (Ephesians vi 6).

In all this, Paul is in the same situation in which every

Christian should find himself, living the natural dialectic between body and soul, and the still further dialectic between the City of Man and the City of God. But this was not all. Paul was caught between two additional worlds: he was both Christian and Jew, a Jewish Christian, and, in being so and facing up to his position here, was more like his Master than those who had not this particular dialogue of Jew and Christian to listen to continually inside their own consciousness. It is chiefly his frank preoccupation with this tension in his life, his flaunting of it, that makes Paul the great symbol of a man between two worlds—a symbol of a man between *any* two worlds, for the Christian-Jewish axis is the great axis set in motion at the center of creation by the passion, death, and resurrection of Our Lord and Savior Jesus Christ. Let us see how Paul himself moves along this axis.

Paul calls himself frankly an "apostle of the gentiles," and yet in doing so implicitly asserts that he is not a gentile (any more than His Master was), but a Hebrew sent *to* the gentiles. For the very concept of gentile is a concept Hebraic in origin, defined quite simply as non-Hebrew. Paul's attitude toward his fellow men and toward the propagation of the faith is inevitably all set in a Hebrew-and-non-Hebrew frame of reference. This frame of reference *is* Paul. What is distinctive of Paul is that he uses this opposition between himself and others (which is a refraction of a cleavage within himself) not to separate himself from others but as a mediating device, to bring himself closer to others, and thereby closer to himself—all this because he is close to His Master, Christ Jesus, Who is Himself both man and God.

Paul's attitudes and evangelizing techniques are as unmistakably and unblushingly dialectical as Kierkegaard's thought processes or the prose style of John Donne's *Meditations*. Paul is a back-and-forth man. The first Christians were all Jewish. But, unlike some of them, Paul did not consider

Christian revelation to be for Jews alone. Hence, repulsed in his preaching by the majority of Jews, he turns to the gentiles. But he is not exclusive here either. When he turns to the gentiles, it is not simply for their sake but also for the sake of his fellow Jews. "For I say to you Gentiles: As long, indeed, as I am an apostle of the Gentiles, I will honor my ministry, in the hope that I may provoke to jealousy *those who are my flesh* [that is, the Jews] *and may save some of them*" (Romans xi 13–14, emphasis added). Paul has evidently the intention of keeping going the dialogue between Jew and gentile, now that he has the ear of both camps.

But this is not all. If he is going to use his work with the gentiles to convert the Jews, he is also going to use the case of the Jews to keep the converted gentiles in line. Once they are converted—and Christians do well to remind themselves that they are all converts, for no one is born a Christian—the gentiles find themselves in a position curiously like that of God's formerly chosen people, liable to rejection by God.

"But if some of the branches [that is, some of the Jews] have been broken off, and if thou, being a wild olive, are grafted in their place, and hast become a partaker of the stem and fatness of the olive tree, do not boast against the branches. But if thou dost boast, still it is not thou that supportest the stem, but the stem thee. Thou wilt say, then, 'Branches were broken off that I might be grafted in.' True, but they were broken off because of unbelief, whereas thou by faith standest. Be not high-minded, but fear. For if God has not spared the natural branches, perhaps he may not spare thee either." [Romans xi 17–21]

A branch remains a branch, something in need of support, and something in constant danger of being broken off. The Christians are now in the same state of danger which occasioned the fall of many Jews.

Thus Paul plays Jew against gentile, as he had played gentile against Jew. But note that he keeps them distinct. Like God Himself, the Master of history, Paul respects differences. He does not want to identify Jew with gentile, any more than he wants to identify man with woman, although he does say elsewhere that these differences, real though they are culturally and sexually, count for nothing in the Kingdom of God, where the reward is based on other considerations entirely (Galatians iii 28). Yet in the Kingdom of God, Paul forever will remain a Jew—a Jew known for his devotion to gentiles, a Roman citizen, and a citizen of Tarsus, which the whole world will then know was "no mean city," and a citizen of the eternal Kingdom of God. He will remain a Jew who has realized the destiny of his people by going out to others, by keeping open the avenues of communication, by cultivating the very opposite of the ghetto mentality, by becoming one in Christ with those who were profoundly other than himself.

Paul was quite aware of the strangely two-sided, dialectical quality of the thinking which makes for his kind of openmindedness and open-heartedness. He was aware, not as speculatively as we are today and yet quite really, of the dialectical quality of God's dealings with men. The Jews, God's chosen people, had been chosen with the knowledge that they would be rejected, rejected because they—that is, many of them, not by any means all of them—had chosen to reject the resurrection of the crucified Redeemer Whom God had chosen for them and Whom God had chosen to be rejected.

Here we are not playing with words. We are touching on the profoundest mysteries of God's action in history. St. Paul thinks and writes in this very manner in the same passage from his Letter to the Romans which we have just cited: "For if the rejection of them [that is, the Jews] is the reconciliation of the world, what will the reception of them be but life from the dead?" Rejection is reconciliation, death is life, and folly is wisdom—that is the typical back-and-forth, dialectical movement of Pauline thought, which in St. Paul's letters is taken up by God Himself to become His own revealed word. This back-and-forth movement, this questing of the man who is not committed to anything save Christ turns St. Paul's own betwixt-and-between situation into a tactical advantage. It is the movement which keeps Paul's preaching open and fecund till the end of time in the minds of those who receive God's word through His Church. It will be recognized again in many saints. This movement, as Père Gaston Fessard has recently pointed out in great detail in *La dialectique des Exercices spirituels,* gives the characteristic structure to St. Ignatius Loyola's famous rule of *tantum . . . quantum,* or "just so much . . . as," whereby we are urged to measure every created thing against something which is other than itself but which refers to it, that is, by God's will concerning it—"just so much of X as will be for the greater glory of God," greater glory, that is, than if there were a little more of X or a little less of X. It is dialectical movement of this sort which makes God's word live and move in our own lives. In St. Paul such a movement registers in his thought and mirrors in his own personal situation.

III

What we can here call St. Paul's dialectical situation—or situations, since he is, as we have seen, caught not between just two worlds, but between several sets of two worlds each —certainly exercised a profound appeal on Father Hecker and his companions, who were to name their new institute with St. Paul's name. Fathers Hecker, Hewit, Deshon, and Baker were every one of them converts—that is, in the usual sense that they had been received into the Church in adult life. These men had all had a good bit of intensive religious formation outside the living body of the Church. They were converts not from paganism, but from Protestantism. And Protestantism, although it is not at all the same as Judaism, still is like Judaism in this: the sincere Protestant possesses part of divine revelation, but not all. To enter into his full heritage in the Church, he has to bring what he already has, if not exactly to fulfillment, as in the case of the Jew, at least to a kind of completeness.

We think naturally of Cardinal Newman here, for Newman testified, as many other converts from Protestantism have done, that the spirituality which he was able, with God's grace, to develop in the bosom of the Church had its real beginnings in his early Protestant life, although it could come to maturity only in the Catholic Church. Moreover, we have Newman's own word associating him with Father Hecker. At Father Hecker's death, Newman wrote that he felt a "sort of unity in our lives—that we had both begun a work of the same kind, he in America and I in England." And yet, being an American, Father Hecker was in one important respect quite different from Newman: his immediate cultural background was more complicated. This fact, too, made Father Hecker's case and that of his associates more like that of St. Paul, if we contrast St. Paul with the early St. Peter—the Simon Peter of Galilee, not the same Simon Peter grown somewhat into the culture of Antioch and Rome. Here, on a still further score, we find St. Paul a man between two worlds—this time, still another two worlds.

St. Paul had been not only a Jew but also a citizen of Tarsus and thus of the Roman Empire, even before he became a Christian. This meant that his Jewish national culture had undergone a further development which had left him not less a Jew but certainly a more complicated person than a Palestinian Jew, such as St. Peter had been. Paul was a

Graeco-Roman Jew. In a somewhat similar way, the culture of the early Paulists was not purely European. It was European culture which had cut itself off from its roots and set itself to grow in a new land, to undergo experiences which Europeans in Europe would not know. It was, in other words, American culture—not a new culture, as we are often inclined to think, but a very old culture, old with the ages of its development in Europe, an old culture which had taken on a new life at the price of acquiring not a new simplicity but a new complexity.

As many misunderstandings which beset Paul of Tarsus were frequently misunderstandings between Palestinian Judaism and the Judaism of the Diaspora, so most of the misunderstandings which beset Father Hecker and his companions at certain critical periods of their lives and which, we know from Father Hecker's own writing and remarks, did so much to bring him closer to God, can be put down as in one way or another misunderstandings between Europe and America—here meaning by America the United States.

We Americans are caught in a kind of dilemma by our own culture. We cannot help being European—and this even if we should be Americans whose ancestors did not come from Europe, for the dominant culture in which America is formed is at root European. And yet we are not European, for every one of us of European stock is descended from persons who turned their backs on Europe, who ran away from their problems. The fact that they may have thought of America as "the land of opportunity" does not alter the fact that they solved a great many of the problems with which they were faced in their homeland by getting away from them, always, in the process, leaving other loved persons behind.

The ancestors of many Americans were brought here by force, either as slaves or as prisoners of one sort or another. But we all too often forget that even for those who did not come here by force the decision to emigrate was an agonizing decision. It may most often have been a very wise decision, but it left its mark on those who came to America, as it certainly left its mark on those left behind. This mark is still to be seen in the complex of attitudes which Americans have toward Europe and Europeans toward Americans. It is easy to understand how, to the European psyche, America remains the symbol of irresponsibility, and how to the American psyche Europe remains the symbol of a cultural impasse and hopeless stagnation.

Neither symbol, of course, has much real application. The European's symbol of America is his justification for not being here, for sticking to his guns instead of running away. The American's symbol of Europe is his justification for leaving it. It may be that he has left it only vicariously, in his ancestors, perhaps ten or twelve generations ago. But Europe is still present in his soul. Every summer this presence draws thousands upon thousands of Americans eastward across the Atlantic to refresh their corporate memories and to prove, in some vague sort of way, that they are not irresponsible, that they really do care—or, in the case of many, that they or their ancestors were right and that Europe is, after all, a very stupid place populated by stupid and incompetent people.

It has been said that all important American novels deal in one way or another with the relation of the American psyche to Europe. Certainly the most important American poetry has grown out of a dialogue with Europe. Americans must live with this dialogue if they are to realize their own potentialities. For there is no place for us to grow out of other than our real selves, and Europe is part of our real selves. There can be no doubt of the fact that an interior dialogue with Europe formed, matured, and finally opened up to all the world the characteristic American attitudes of

Father Hecker. Reared in America, converted to the Catholic Church in America, he felt intensely from the beginning the need for the Church to be at home in his native land. Yet he went to Belgium for his novitiate. And the Paulist community was actually first conceived in Europe—to be precise, in Rome. Furthermore, it was no sooner founded than a European branch was projected—although such development proved for the time being not to be part of God's designs for His new band of missionaries.

The significant thing, however, about Father Hecker's dialogue with Europe as with everyone else is its open, developing character. Father Hecker did not work back and forth between Europe and America to make Europeans Americans or Americans Europeans. Indeed, strange as it may seem, constant involvement in the European-American problem in his case only opened his field of vision more and more to horizons beyond both Europe and America, as St. Paul's dialogue between the Jew within him and the Graeco-Roman citizen within him only enlarged his horizons to make him the Apostle not merely of Graeco-Romans but of the entire gentile, as well as the Jewish, world. The enlarging international vision which grew in Father Hecker's mind can be seen in a fascinating passage from his private memoranda written in Europe during his illness in 1874 and 1875:

What else has been my exile from home for unless to prepare my soul to make my life-experience applicable to the general condition of the Church and the world in its present crisis? The past was for the United States, the future, for the world. To this end all particular attachments to persons, places, labors, had to be cut off, not to give a bias to the judgment, and not to interfere with my action. It was with a deeper meaning than at first sight appeared to me that I now see why I called myself "An International Catholic."

Father Hecker might well have written that it was with a deeper meaning than at first sight appeared to him that he now saw why he and those associated with him called his institute the Paulists. How explicitly he and those around him were initially aware of the full applicability of the symbol which they had snatched from real history, the symbol of St. Paul, Jewish Christian and Apostle of Christianity to the non-Jewish world, we perhaps shall never know. For in this brief treatment, or in a treatment much longer, we cannot hope to plumb the full depths of this mysterious personage who made real to the new Christians the old Hebrew prophetic vision of a converted heathendom. But we do see here how intimately, in Father Hecker's mind, the formation of a Paulist and of "an international Catholic" go hand in hand.

IV

Father Hecker's international outlook is a lesson for American Catholics today—and all the more because it was so immediately and urgently a genuine product of the American scene. The vocation of the Paulist, or of any Catholic today, is not to be exclusive, not to be provincial, parochial, but to be open, conciliatory, unifying, vis-à-vis the entirety of the human race. Our aim is to win all men without exception to Christ. If they reject us, we have no time to waste in denunciations, any more than St. Paul did, for we must turn to others with the hope that this may help us to win those from whom for a time we have had to turn away. The Catholic vision is a vision which opens lines of communication between men, not one which closes them. The desire to close them, to keep to ourselves, to keep "pure" of any defilement by avoiding contact with those different from us has impeded the preaching of the Gospel in the past and impedes it today. This is the mentality of the unconverted Jew, of Saul of Tarsus, who does not want the salvation of the nations, the *goyim,* but only his own salvation and that of his people. The converted Jew, the Jewish Christian, Paul of Tarsus, is no such isolationist.

These are matters for urgent thought on the part of American Catholics. We have known in American history various "nativist" movements, attempts to make American civilization fold back on itself, refuse contact with other civilizations, and even eliminate some of its most distinctive and valuable parts in order to achieve or preserve an imagined "purity" which has no foundation whatsoever in fact and history. Catholics have themselves suffered from these movements—the Know-Nothings, the American Protective Association, the Ku Klux Klan. But today American Catholics themselves can, it seems, be taken in by these movements. Of late the press has reported that they have been invited in some places to join the Ku Klux Klan. And invitations of this sort would not be issued had not some Catholics given signs of favoring certain principles of isolation—national, cultural, racial, or religious—for which such an organization is known to stand.

The opposition of the United States to international Communism, while certainly necessary and desirable, creates as a side effect a climate in which isolationism can flourish. Many American Catholics, it is sadly evident, are all too prone to lump together the opposition of the Church to Communism and the opposition of our government to Communism. In Europe one encounters with fair regularity the American Catholic who resents the fact that the episcopacy of the country where he finds himself does not publicly endorse American anti-Communist foreign policy and shows little enthusiasm for the United States military forces. Certainly Communism must be opposed on both the religious and the politico-military fronts, but the fronts are not to be identified. It is to be noted that the Holy See has tried desperately to keep open certain avenues of communication with the Communist countries at times when our national government has had to favor closing some areas of communication with which it has to deal. The religious outlook here is, in important respects, more "open" than the political, and necessarily so.

Although the Church is unique in her possession of the full truth of divine revelation, there is nothing isolationist about her possession of it. And because the word "exclusive" can hardly be effectively dissociated from the notion of isolationism, it would seem better not to speak of the Church's "exclusive" claim to truth. The Church does not want to exclude anyone. Whatever excluding there is, is all done from the outside. Yet we American Catholics are not free of exclusivist tendencies. I recall the present distress of a group of religious dedicated to work for the conversion of the Jews in the face of the built-in anti-Semitism of Catholic as well as Protestant groups which, they frankly state, directly hampers their apostolate. Those of us who work with American Negroes or are perhaps Negroes ourselves know all too well the racial exclusivism of the great bulk of American Catholics, who prove quite indistinguishable here on the whole from non-Catholic Americans. On the international scale our recent record as Americans, if not as Catholics, is not enviable. Among Western nations we Americans score the very lowest of all in the proportion of the recent Hungarian refugees, for example, to whom we have granted asylum. And we score lowest both in terms of our total national income and in terms of our total population. Despite their own devastation by war, England and France and Germany have of late years been the refuge of the oppressed on a much more generous scale than the United States has been. And few American Catholics seem discontented with this state of affairs.

And how do American Catholics stand on the foreign missions? Have we begun to match the past generosity here of the European nations at a time when they were much less prosperous than we? Or do we restrict our aid to monetary contributions—the easiest kind of aid there is—instead of inspiring ourselves to give ourselves wholly and entirely to other peoples, to give of our manpower, and that for good, out of the love of Christ?

How far can an American Catholic foreign missionary afford to identify himself with the countries to which he is sent? How far will he be hampered by the American attitude that it is all right for other persons to renounce citizenship to their country, no matter what that country may be, in order to become an American citizen, but that for an American to become identified permanently with some other people in such a way as to become one of them is somehow despicable and, indeed, beneath the exalted dignity of this chosen people of God? American Catholics have been sensitive to the alleged chauvinism of missionaries from other countries. But we certainly have a built-in chauvinism of our own, at least back at home here, where it seems chauvinistic for missionaries of other countries to teach *their* language and *their* culture but where one hopes and even takes for granted that American missionaries are teaching English and, of course, introducing baseball.

Father Hecker and his companions found that it took work to overcome isolationism and exclusivism in all its forms. It took work not only to open the minds of our separated Protestant brethren to the truths of Catholic faith, but also to open the minds of Catholics to maintain the necessary contacts which the permanent mission of the Church makes imperative. Even today, when on so many diverse fronts advances in communication have put men all over the surface of the globe more in touch with one another than ever before, we have still to remind ourselves that it takes work to keep man's mind open, and specifically to keep the American Catholic's mind open—to keep it in vital contact with the world around it, with the non-Catholic world in the United States and with the non-American world, Catholic and non-Catholic, outside the United States. If the notion of mission, of being sent to bring the Gospel, the Good News, means anything in Catholic tradition—and it means everything, being no less than an extension of the Incarnation and ultimately of the Procession of the Second Person of the Blessed Trinity from the Father—we can have no isolationists among us. But men's minds are not naturally open. They almost seem naturally to be closed, as St. Paul and the early Paulists often found to their sorrow.

"What is the fundamental idea of the Paulists?" asks Father Hecker in the same private memoranda from which we quoted earlier:

> It is the idea of organizing the practical side of the Church in view of the needs of the age and the triumph of religion, for the greatest expansion of the ideal Christian life possible. What is the ideal Christian life? It is human nature in its entire force, sanctified and transformed by Christianity.

This ideal, of "human nature in its *entire* force, sanctified and transformed by Christianity," is an outgrowth of Catholicity as incarnate in America, but it is congenial to Catholicity everywhere. There is nothing restrictively American in it at all. Insofar as it is an inspiration to American Catholics, it is an invitation to them to realize their greatest potentialities by getting outside themselves, by thinking with the rest of the human race through thinking with the Church.

There is no real human culture which is isolated. Being human, any culture is destined in one way or another to belong ultimately to all men, and to come to fruition through Christ—through Him and with Him and in Him. The Church thrives and grows in cultures which have this outward, upward, forward, positive thrust, for she herself has a comparable, if greater and supernatural, thrust. She is a growing organism—Christ's Mystical Body. The American in Father Hecker made him revel a little in the idea of growth and progress. This love of growth and progress, however, is a mark not merely of his American heritage, but also, at another level, of his Catholic instinct. For the ideals of growth and progress are among the most powerful religious forces, if not the most powerful, characteristic of our age.

Moreover, these ideals are closely related to the concept of Catholicity itself. This can be seen when we contrast the concept of "Catholic" with that which is often said to be its equivalent, the concept "universal." It is noteworthy that the Church herself, even when speaking Latin, has consistently referred to herself and thought of herself by means of the Greek-formed concept *katholikos* rather than by means of the Latin-based term universal, *universalis*. The concepts share a certain amount of meaning, but not their whole meaning, and even that which they share is oriented differently in the two cases.

"Universal," or *universalis* in Latin, has its roots in two Latin terms, *unum,* or "one," and *vertere,* or "to turn." It designates some kind of wholeness or inclusiveness. But it designates this wholeness in terms of some kind of turning, a turning around, perhaps, as one might describe a whole circle by turning around a point, or a turning of many things into one. In either event, there is something negative about the concept. A turning of many things into one means some denial of their individual identities. The describing of a circle around a point means the marking of a limit. A circle is inclusive, but it is inclusive in a limiting way: what is inside its perimeter is included, what is outside is positively excluded. Some construct such as this can be seen in operation when for example we use the term "universal" as applying to "universal ideas." A universal idea or concept is one which in its own oneness includes all the members of a class. "Include" means, at root, "close in." The universal concept closes in the members of a class, and it does so in part by *ex*cluding the nonmembers. The same negative factor appears more or less operative in the other common uses of universal as designating that which is inclusive, that which "takes in" a whole "field," or which "extends" to certain limits.

One might think that there is no remedy for this type of conceptualization, that man must think of things this way, that the penalty of finite existence is a certain negative quality in all thought. And yet the negative quality is not so operative in the concept "catholic." *Katholikos* in Greek means literally "through-the-whole." The concept has a positive, outgoing quality to it. Instead of pulling things in around a center, it moves out to all things. In the concept of catholic, "through-the-whole," there is here no hint of fencing in. Rather, what is catholic floods being with itself. Let being grow, expand, as much as you will, what is Catholic will grow and expand with it, filling its every nook and cranny.

This is why Catholic love, or more particularly Catholic faith, Catholic hope, and Catholic charity have an expansive, positive quality as against the pinched, impoverished, forced, and quite unpersuasive "universal" love for "universal" mankind in this "universal" frame of the universe which man of the Enlightenment liked to profess. The universalist is betrayed by the history of the concept which he has laid hold of: he wishes to pull things in to himself. The Catholic wants to give himself to others, to go out to them in an expansive movement of love, even more than E. E. Cummings' father who "moved through dooms of love . . . singing each new leaf out of each tree."

It thus seems not too far from a love of what is Catholic to a love of what is growing and progressing. For growth and progress are "expansive" notions, too. Like Catholicism itself, these are not negative notions, but essentially positive and open.

Thus it is that Father Hecker's positive approach to reality, his interest in the spread of the Kingdom, his humble understanding of the movements of grace in his own life as positive forward movements conducive to spiritual growth, has something uncompromisingly Catholic about it. He catches something of the spirit of the Catholic Church, and certainly much of St. Paul, in writing on one of his own anniversaries, August 2, 1864:

> Today is the twentieth anniversary of my baptism and reception into the Holy Church. To me my life has been one continued growth; and hence I have never had any desire to return to any part or period of it. This applies as well to my life before I was received into the Church as after. My best life was always in the present.

In the present, looking into the future—the future where Father Hecker and his companions dreamed of the conversion of all America and all the world to Christ. There may be something youthful in this enthusiasm, and there is certainly something buoyant. But buoyancy and a permanently youthful enthusiasm are certainly part of St. Paul's own complex character, as they are part of the Catholic tradition, and that outside America, too.

The early Paulists' dream brought them the cross of Christ in many ways. And at this they were not in the least surprised. They bore the cross as we all should, not by retiring more and more into themselves, but by opening themselves up more and more, keeping clear all avenues of communication possible so as to bring Christ to all men as far as under God's grace they could.

4
Secular Knowledge and Revealed Religion

An understanding of the kind of presence which the Church exercises in the world demands some sense of the relationship between divine revelation and natural knowledge. Studies in the history of ideas, that is to say the history of the concepts and judgments which man has learned to form through the life of the human race, have made it impossible to retain some of the earlier notions of this relationship. Earlier, we might have been tempted to think of natural knowledges as existing, more or less preformed, by themselves and of divine revelation as superimposed on these knowledges from without.

Such a picture will never do. When public divine revelation destined for all mankind was begun, it was only after mankind had been developing its store of knowledge for thousands upon thousands of years. Initially, this revelation was given in a definite culture, that of the Hebrews. Now, in any culture knowledge is possessed by a network of concepts and judgments which are intricately related to one another and dependent upon one another. Each culture has its own network of concepts which registers in the particular development of language concomitant with the culture and which is in part determined by this development.

A single individual could not begin to elaborate for himself the concepts which it has taken the branch of human culture into which he is born thousands upon thousands of years to elaborate and which he learns through this culture as he matures. For knowledge is not something accumulated in the human mind by a kind of addition or accretion comparable to the hooking of additional freight cars onto a train. Real increase in knowledge involves learning how to form new concepts and thus new judgments capable of establishing the knowledge in one's mind. One's ability to form new concepts is dependent upon the concepts one has already learned to form. The concepts one has learned to form will depend in turn upon the culture or cultures with which one is in contact. Not that they will not depend on "things" or on "reality." But one cannot simply take in "things" or reality in one fell swoop. One must be taught within a linguistic and cultural context the places where it is possible to take hold of reality. The child must be coached in forming concepts. The number of concepts—to speak somewhat analogously, for it is not quite possible to count concepts—which can be formed vis-à-vis reality is potentially infinite. Each culture narrows the field by specializing in certain types of awarenesses and neglecting others.

Of course, these specializations or cultures are not mutually exclusive. A Western European, with the specializations in viewing reality which his culture has opened to him, can learn to think like a Tibetan or a Yapese if he wishes to put forth the effort. Many do put forth such effort to learn, at least in part, what another culture is like from inside. Indeed, in our day intercultural understanding is becoming possible with less and less effort as cultures themselves grow together into a kind of world-wide culture with an always quickening pace through the naturally accelerated development of communications which marks the stage to which human society has by our age evolved. Yet even this newer and more encompassing culture which is shaping itself slowly but inexorably before our eyes is still a culture. It will represent some sort of specialization, if a broader specialization. More important, it will have a history, and a more complex history, the more it represents the unification of diverse cultural developments.

Thus, today and tomorrow, as yesterday, any human intellectual activity must take place in a special culture. All man's intellectual acquisitions are lodged within a particular culture which gives them characteristics of its own and makes them datable. The most abstract philosophical disquisitions, like the most topical literary creations, bear in themselves the mark of time. Given sufficient knowledge of the history of ideas and forms of expression, they can all be dated.

Divine revelation, too, appears within a culture, within a certain specialized frame of reference, where it has certain special time marks associated with it. Thus, even independently of the personal Incarnation of the Second Person of the Blessed Trinity, the Son of God and the Word of God, if we could conceive of a divine revelation consisting of abstract principles, some kind of "incarnation" would be necessary even for these, although in such cases it would be more accurate to speak of a "lodging" or "grounding" than of an "incarnation." For the abstract principles would have to be set forth in a going language and network of thought, attaching themselves to what a particular culture knew and foregoing the types of manifestations which would require concepts and awarenesses which the culture did not have. This condition of human knowledge is in a way dealt with by Jaspers through his concept of "encompassing," and was dealt with by the ancient Greeks through their related concept of the aphorism, that is, the "bounding" or "horizoning" of a truth (for this strange term historically derives from the same original as our term "horizon").

This means that there is no way for even the divine message to enter into the human mind without entangling itself in a whole network of interrelated knowledges and in the sociology of a people. But it means more than this. For if the development of knowledges and of sociological structure is part of the divine plan, divine revelation does not become entangled with networks of interrelated human knowledge and with concrete human culture for lack of something better. Except for the fact that we are dealing with a revelation which is more than natural, which is connected not with man's birth (*natura*) but with his rebirth in Christ, we might say that cultures and networks of knowledge are the natural habitat of revelation. Since we cannot quite say this, we shall say that God wished His revelation to be lodged within cultures and networks of knowledge, and not that it be made in any other fashion—if any other fashion would be even possible. In Old Testament language, by revelation God "has pitched his tent among us," and the name of His Son, Who is Himself God and God's Word, God's Revelation, is Emmanuel, "God *with* us."

But this "lodging" of God's Revelation among us means something further still. For God is the Master of history, and as cultures grow and differentiate and, after initial differentiation, finally more and more converge through the course of history, aspects of His Revelation become evident which were not evident before. God intends His Revelation to bear a dynamic relationship to history. This, we might suspect, is why He was content with a revelation made at a certain point in history by Jesus Christ and not to be added to after the death of the last apostle. It was quite enough to have this Revelation planted at one point in history. It was a seed. From here it would grow.

II

When we consider, then, the interaction of revealed truth and of the theology derivative from revealed truth with the various secular disciplines, we can by no means picture the nonreligious as developing in some never-never land by themselves, of religion and theology as developing by themselves, and of a kind of commuting movement between the two "fields." All the knowledges which a man enjoys cohabit in the same human mind, and they do not establish themselves there in any neat sequence. Revelation is given within a going network of human thought which is actively developing at the time Revelation is made. And this Revelation is not made all at once, but over many hundreds of years, terminating with the life of Jesus, Who Himself manifested Himself gradually to His apostles and to the world, and Whose manifestation was understood even more gradually than it was made, coming clear to the apostles only after His death, at Pentecost.

It is thus, as a matter of fact, often more of a challenge to be asked where one discipline does not influence another and does not influence theology than to be asked where it does. Studies in the history of ideas have detailed many of the ways in which the pattern of thinking in any age and culture tends in many profound ways to be of a piece, even when we have to do with knowledge of quite diverse "fields." Favorite ways of thinking, thought "models," move unsupervised from one field of activity in the mind to another field and then, in sometimes modified forms, back again. Leo Spitzer has recently remarked how our biological and sociological concept of "environment" was coined by Carlyle (not without earlier analogues in the English language to make the coinage workable), who built upon Goethe's notion of the *Umwelt*, which in turn mirrors Newton's idea of the "circumambient medium," primarily a concept for use in physics. We might have a different sociology if we had not exploited this particular way of conceiving sociological phenomena by analogy with now extinct physical theories. Or we might have a different physics, which is to say that we might know certain things about physics which today we do not know and we might not know certain things we do, if scientific thinking had not started off with and so elaborately exploited the Greek concept of the atom, *atomos*, the uncuttable one, which still influences our way of thinking about matter today.

In the field of theology, the Covenant theories of William Perkins, William Ames, and other writers favored by our early New England Puritans make use of the legalism and of views concerning free agreements or contracts which had proved so serviceable in the Puritan's bourgeois commercial world. In a similar way, the pastor of a Catholic parish in today's United States will refer to the parish's wonderful educational "plant" which "turns out" a fine "product," making use of the frames of reference familiar to a technological and industrial society. The Protestant (or Catholic) clergyman thinks often enough of "selling" his congregation "on" the Gospel, utilizing concepts which have proved serviceable in a commercial culture. And anyone who characterizes Billy Graham's work as a religious "drive" is exploiting an outlook given currency by the Newtonian physics of "forces," which were supposed to account for movement in the universe.

In none of these cases is there an evident and conscious attempt to import the apparatus or findings of secular knowledge into religion and theology. One simply thinks of religion and theology in terms current more or less in all fields. "Turning out products" and "drives" represent concepts applied to religious movements, emotional activity, physical energy, social aggressiveness, and an indefinite number of other things. These are thought models which are part of the ordinary furniture of the contemporary mind.

The number of thought models which are popular in any one age and culture can, of course, be very great and their interrelation more complicated than the most thoroughgoing explanation will ever have time to show. Still, certain models or clusters of models are the hallmarks of certain ages. For models come and go. Not that the old ones turn out necessarily to be untrue. They may remain entirely true while they become quite unfruitful. Models provide analogies which are of their very nature limited, and, as the dialogue which makes human society what it is moves on, the models once found serviceable because relevant in a special way to current preoccupations are abandoned for others more relevant to new problems, new insights, and new solutions.

There are, of course, occasional deliberate borrowings by one field of knowledge from another. And occasionally great progress in one field will immediately and inevitably make for great progress in another. Thus the archeological studies of the past century and a half have revolutionized Biblical theology. But when one looks at the relationships of the various disciplines in their larger aspects and over larger periods of time, it becomes apparent that the contributions of one discipline to another are subordinate to the more pervasive, mysterious movements which somehow affect all disciplines.

As an example of a large pervasive movement, Alfred North Whitehead and others have rightly made much of the relationship between the Hebraeo-Christian heritage and the spectacular development of science in modern times. For it is a fact that what we know as modern science, those knowledges which have emerged in connection with the application of mathematics to physics, have only one starting point in the long history of the human race: Western Europe after the scholastic experience of the Middle Ages. Medieval scholasticism was marked by an unshakable conviction that scientific and philosophical answers to questions can be found, that the world is understandable in one way or another. Medieval science and philosophy were not always very adequate, but they can hardly be said to have lacked confidence. In the intensity of its conviction that everything can be explained, as Whitehead observes, medieval scholasticism outstrips even Greek rationalism as seen, for example, in Aristotle. Aristotle did not believe that the world was created by God or that its history was ruled by Him and consequently could not avoid the haunting implication that ultimately there were aspects of reality which lay outside all explanation in sheer chaos.

It was different in the rationalism developed out of the Greek rationalism within the Hebraic and Christian traditions. Here all being outside God Himself is made by Him. Since God acts intelligently, being Intelligence Itself, the medieval Christian could assume that all reality must be somehow or other intelligible. The quest of understanding may often be long and arduous, but it is to medieval man generally a worth-while quest and a feasible one. But if the medieval world view is a cradle of modern science, it is also a cradle of our scientific theology. Medieval theological explanation is of a special kind, but there is no mistaking the fact that, as compared with other theological traditions, it thinks of itself as scientific in a way in which earlier theologies did not. Most medieval theologians did not agree with St. Thomas Aquinas in holding that theology was a strict science, but the drive to approximate a strict science is evident through the entire theological development of the period. Here there is less question of the "influence" of one discipline on another than of the development of various disciplines in the same intellectual climate out of undifferentiated sources.

III

If we view the "contributions" of the various disciplines to religion and theology in terms of some of the more pervasive, mysterious movements which form part of the general evolution of the cosmos and of human understanding rather than in terms of specific and calculated borrowings or exchanges, what can be said about the pattern of interaction in the Christian era up to the present time?

For convenience, we can restrict ourselves to the West, for the picture in the East and in all Africa except the northern portions, while perhaps even more interesting, is more complicated. Christianity—which we must remember has come to every culture, including the West, from outside—has made initial effective contact with great areas of Eastern and African culture in a later historical setting of incredible complexity, that in which the East and the West have been moving closer and closer together as the human consciousness over the entire face of the earth becomes more and more "globalized."

In the West, three great periods of interaction between the nonreligious or secular disciplines and Christianity can conveniently be distinguished, although I should not wish to suggest that no other convenient grouping of periods can be hit upon. The first period was that in which the Christian religion assimilated the rhetorical tradition which dominated the formal education of the ancient Greek and Roman. (It must be remembered here that interest in philosophy in a purportedly nonrhetorical framework, an interest deriving through Socrates, Plato, and Aristotle, was, as H. I. Marrou has shown in *L'histoire de l'éducation dans l'antiquité*, subordinate to rhetoric both in origin and in over-all influence.) The Greek Fathers of the Church—St. John Chrysostom, St. Gregory Nazianzen, St. Basil, St. Gregory of Nyssa, and others—and the Latin Fathers, particularly St. Augustine and St. Jerome, utilized the linguistically oriented learning of the rhetorical tradition for explicating and otherwise dealing with Hebraic and Christian revelation.

This rhetorical tradition has proved invaluable to the development of Christian doctrine and Christian asceticism. For a rhetorically centered education is one centered on communication, and thus, wittingly or unwittingly, upon persons and personal relations. The rhetorical tradition was not without an interest in science. Indeed, it was the womb of all modern science. But in it science was not thought of in an a-social setting. Any science was a "doctrine," a "teaching," something communicated by a teacher to an audience. Today we do not think of physics, for example, as this sort of thing (although we could quite validly). By the rhetorically oriented ancient Greek and Roman world, all knowledge was felt much more strongly than by us, as existing in a personal context.

This context made secular learning in a special way congenial to Christians. Hebrew and Christian revelation is the revelation of a personal God, Who takes a personal interest in man and Whose will governs history and sometimes even breaks through history's expected patterns. Judaism and Christianity (and to some extent Mohammedanism, which derives from them) make more of prayer than do other religions. Indeed, in a sense their religious activity is entirely prayer, that is, communication, communal and personal, with a living, personal God. Judaism and Christianity are thus, in a sense, rhetorical religions. Other religions have somewhat other orientations. For example, Hinduism and Buddhism make a religious practice of yoga, a discipline directing the attention not to a person but to an object—a genuine depersonalizing mechanism, which, in Tantric Buddhism especially, utilizes for contemplation geometric figures such as mandalas or magic circles. This sort of practice—in reality a practice antedating Hinduism and Buddhism, as the study of grammar, dialectic, and rhetoric antedates Christianity—has never proved congenial to Christianity, which has found the rhetorical tradition, by contrast, a gold mine for ascetical and theological development.

The rhetorical tradition has been one of the strong factors in the development of the prayers of the Church's liturgy from the very beginning. But its influence is not limited to formal, oral prayers or to the early ages of Christianity. It affects even highly individual, private mental prayer, such as that which is encouraged by the *Spiritual Exercises* of St. Ignatius Loyola, the sixteenth century ascetical treatise which derives from a long-growing tradition and is in more widespread use today by Catholics, clerical and lay, than ever before. In the *Spiritual Exercises* the procedure for keeping the mind and affections at work during prayer is highly reminiscent of the rhetoricians' prescriptions for finding material for discourse.

Among those who do not have a firsthand knowledge of the *Spiritual Exercises,* there is a tendency to consider them as a routine something like yoga. Indeed, a recent article in a well-known national news magazine made them out to be something very like this. The fact is that, as has just been hinted in a brilliant book by Père Gaston Fessard, *La dialectique des Exercices spirituels,* the exercises which St. Ignatius Loyola proposes are really a dialogue or a "talk" between man and his Creator. The presence of a "director" (called the "retreat master" by modern American retreatants) for those following the Exercises, and the fact that he *talks* with the exercitants not with a view to indoctrinating them but with a view to facilitating their own personal dialogue with God, advertises the dialogue setting of the Exercises, and thus their rhetorical cast. Indeed, even in its highest and mystical forms, which the *Spiritual Exercises* would encourage in the exercitant as far as is compatible with grace, prayer for the Christian remains—indeed, becomes all the more intensely—communication with a personal God.

Another area where rhetoric influences theology and religion can be seen in the Renaissance disputes on the notion of Christian faith. Both the Latin word for faith, *fides,* and the Greek word, *pistis,* had long been in common use as technical rhetorical terms designating the "conviction" which the orator sought to establish in the minds of his hearers. The humanist stress on rhetoric coincides with the great Catholic-Protestant disputes concerning the nature of Christian faith, and it is quite certain that the rhetorical use of the term *fides*—a use thoroughly familiar to all those who had been through a Renaissance school—exerted an influence on the disputants. I know of no study which goes adequately into the question of the rhetorical influence on theology here and propose the question as one which well merits thorough investigation.

The second period of interaction between nonreligious disciplines and religion and theology in the West has already been briefly mentioned. It is that of medieval and Renaissance scholasticism. Those unfamiliar with the curriculum of the medieval university might think that it is redundant to speak of the contribution of scholasticism to religion and theology for the reason that scholasticism was concerned with nothing else. Yet the growing study of the disciplines taught in the Middle Ages by men such as A. C. Crombie, Ernest A. Moody, Philotheus Boehner, I. M. Bochenski, and others shows that scholastic "philosophy" was actually in great part an elaborate physics and a logic developed far beyond Aristotle's in the direction of a quantified or formal logic such as that of Whitehead, Carnap, and Russell today. As an approach to the entire field of human knowledges which was extraordinarily inquisitive about the secular as well as the sacred, if sometimes badly misguided in its cosmology and physics, scholasticism thus did make contributions to religion and theology of the sort being treated here—contributions building up attitudes of mind and general approaches which are the forerunners of modern science. Scholasticism also acted as a mediator, bringing the ancient rhetorical tradition down to later centuries—for the three ages we are here distinguishing all overlap somewhat and interpenetrate.

The distinctive feature of scholasticism which is of some particular interest here is its scientizing impulse, its tendency to make every discipline in the curriculum feel like a closely integrated body of knowledge of the order of geometry. Scholasticism encouraged an "objective," nonrhetorical view of the universe, and under this aspect can be seen as reaching a kind of maximal effect with the Newtonian age, which, as we now know, both reacted against scholasticism and flowed out of it as a kind of consequence. The Newtonian age, even more decisively than earlier scholastic ages, encouraged a decidedly nonrhetorical, "objective" view of the universe and of all reality. Built on applying to physics the sciences of mathematics, which belong in a visually apprehended universe rather than in a resounding rhetorical world, and upon specialization in "observation" (which meant largely working in space through vision, through the eyes), Newtonian physics had definite effects on man's religious outlook. Intellectual knowledge was now preferably thought of as like that type of sensory knowledge which is had through sight.

Its likeness to that sensory knowledge which is had through hearing, through words, was discounted or even entirely ignored. Since person-to-person communication is basically through voice and sound, the personal element tended to drop out of man's view of the world.

The world of Newtonian physics, it has often been pointed out, was to become a strangely silent one, with sound itself reduced (quite legitimately for certain scientific purposes) to wave lengths—that is, reduced to sight as though sound were really wave patterns on a chart or oscillograph, although such patterns obviously make no sound at all, but are only spatial correlates of sound. The result of this emphasis on the visual was that man, the speaking animal, became himself a kind of surd in the Newtonian world view, which, despite its great success elsewhere, was seriously defective in theories of communication.

For the most part the "substitution theory" of language held the day: words "stood" for things and were thought of as manipulable in space—a notion already far developed in the supposition theory of medieval logic. Thought was felt to be at its best if there were no words connected with it (as though this were possible), and the age spawned all sorts of schemes to reduce the vernaculars to a kind of immobility, such as men were familiar with, to a certain extent, in the Latin in which scientific writing was still done. Control over the spoken word was to be exercised by fixing words once for all in dictionaries and other schemata, by "locating" them where they could be "found" in space.

In this climate it was inevitable that men should tend to accommodate God to their silent world. God's work was preferably likened to that of the architect or the mason, not to that of a speaker. Men tended to forget that voice is the external act which most manifests man's creativity and that, when God is likened to man (as He must be when men talk of Him—for He has to be likened to something, and to what higher being familiar to man can He be likened?), the way to speak of His creative activity most effectively and accurately is to say, as the Scriptures do, that He created with His word. "And God said: Let there be light. And there was light." (Genesis i 13.)

By the seventeenth and eighteenth centuries, tending to think of God as an architect or engineer (and one, moreover, working alone—for the essentially social setting in which all science is learned and exists had been occluded), men were having serious difficulties with the notion of divine revelation. Their whole frame of mind had been conditioned against thinking of God's activity in terms of communication at all. As a result, the mysterious interchange between an "I" and a "Thou" which is implied in all speech tended to disappear, and a Deists' God emerges—a quite convincing figure because He was thought of as a kind of "force" such as one was familiar with from Newtonian physics. The difficulties with the notion of divine revelation which mark the seventeenth, eighteenth, and nineteenth centuries and which begin to diminish with the discovery of evolution and the eclipse of Newtonian physics are undoubtedly due to the way of viewing the universe which produced the Newtonian state of mind (itself, in many ways, an advance over earlier states of mind).

This brings us to the third period of the interaction between nonreligious disciplines and religion and theology in the West, the age which mankind entered definitively in the nineteenth century and which was ushered in by the Romantic movement. This is an age—we are still in it—marked by a tremendous development of biology and of the biological outlook which finally awakened the human consciousness to the significance of the data bearing on evolution.

Elaborated by Darwin, Wallace, and others with reference

to the organic world, the concept of evolution opened a new understanding of the entire cosmos, which, instead of being regarded as a mere aggregate of forces and vectors, was now regarded as like some sort of huge and ancient organism, growing toward a maturity which it had from the beginning contained in germ. In this age sociology, a science with strong biological connections, replaces metaphysics as an approach to the ultimates in human life. August Comte is the new Aristotle. History supersedes mathematics as the discipline promising the most rewarding insights into the movement of things. And sociology and history crossbreed to produce a Hegel and eventually a Marx.

Through Hegel's dialectic, a notion of dialogue between person and person has, subtly at first and not unequivocally, obtruded itself anew into man's philosophical and scientific outlook, making its way (again, not unequivocally) into physics through Einstein and his perceptions regarding the need to take into account the observer (who is always a person) as an integral part of physical data and through the notion of complementarity in atomic physics, which Bohr has described in terms of a physical dialectic (or dialogue). And finally, both as a consequence of Hegel's work and as a reaction against him, at the point of this period at which we live, there has finally developed a philosophy of personalism, more intensely and reflectively sensitive to the demands and significance of the human person than any philosophy has ever been before.

The mentality which had produced these scientific and philosophical developments of course had registered in religious and theological thinking as well. The notion of the Church as the Mystical Body of Christ, a "biological-type" notion which had lain dormant and largely unexploited in Catholic doctrine from the beginning, became during the late nineteenth century and the early twentieth a major interest of Catholic theology. And the related notion of growth toward maturity which is featured in John Henry Newman's closely reasoned work *An Essay on the Development of Christian Doctrine* became the hinge on which a whole religious career as significant as Newman's could turn. Emphasis on the social implications of Christianity grew all through this period, slowly in some Protestant circles, spectacularly fast in others, and quite as irresistibly in Catholic circles, if here at a more measured pace, for integration of this fresh outlook with the already vast complex of Catholic teaching was a delicate and complicated problem.

In this third period, the most profound effect upon religion and theology can best be described as an intensifying of a sense of history. The historical sense has revamped and revitalized Biblical studies, and has led to a new awareness of the peculiarly profound and unique historical orientation of the entire Hebraic and Christian heritage.

The Protestant theologian Oscar Cullmann, the Catholic theologian Jean Daniélou, the cultural psychologist Mircea Eliade, and others have made much of the point that the Jewish and Christian sense of time is "linear" and thus in accord with the evolutionary picture of the world as something which starts in one condition and moves to a quite different condition. Various cyclic theories of the universe, theories of "perpetual return," had proposed that every event we encounter has happened before and is fated to happen over and over again. Such theories use as a model the apparently perpetual recurrence of the seasons. But with the discovery of the evolution of the cosmos it becomes evident that this recurrence is not perpetual. It had a beginning and is moving toward some sort of finish, as are all the phenomena we encounter in the universe. The models which had given cyclicism plausibility are not there. The Jewish and Christian linear or eschatological sense of time thus takes on new importance, exhibiting a profound relevance to the cosmos as this reveals itself in history.

In the contribution of historical studies to the revitalization of the religious outlook, there is evident again the interaction between religion and theology on the one hand and the secular sciences on the other. For, as a matter of fact, the interest in history which has fed back into religious studies today is in its origins largely traceable to the Hebraeo-Christian religious outlook. The Hebrews were a chosen people who realized their religious destiny in and through history. The Christian religion is ushered in by a long and consciously historical preparation through the Hebrew race which is quite unparalleled in the case of other religions and which Christian theology has always considered of major significance. And, although Hegel's philosophy of history is not a straightforward theology, its roots in the Hebraeo-Christian preoccupation with history are unmistakable. Today Communism is imbuing many men who have never known Judaism or Christianity with a sense of history having a strong apocalyptic and echatological torque. But the present Chinese or Viet Minh Communists' fascination with history is not an indigenous product. It was learned from the works of a Jew, Karl Marx, who did his writing in a Christian cultural setting. Modern religion and theology are influenced by the historical bent of secular sciences, but this historical bent itself is a product of a definite religious culture.

A similar interaction between religious and secular knowledges is observable even in the case of the evolutionary outlook, which, of course, is related to the sense of history. Recognition of the phenomenon of evolution demanded a certain orientation of mind. One had to think of the organic world as though it were not a group of more or less detached "natures" each with carefully policed perfections of its own, but rather as though it were somehow one organism engaged in a process of self-perfection, of "making" something of itself, and that against great odds and with effort. Darwin's and Wallace's "natural selection" arose through the "survival of the fittest" in the course of a "struggle."

This view of life as a "struggle" against an Adversary (Satan means Adversary) toward "self-perfection" is a typically Christian view—the view which, if we follow Max Weber, R. H. Tawney, and Amintore Fanfani, was built up in Christian asceticism especially within religious orders. From these it spread through the late Middle Ages and particularly in the sixteenth century to all of bourgeois society to produce throughout great sectors of secular society what David Riesman has called the "inner-directed" man, intent on perfecting his native abilities not by withdrawal from struggle (in Buddhist or Stoic fashion) but by continued personal effort and fight.

Against this historical background, it is fascinating to look into the thought models in pre-Darwinian writings of various sorts, for example in Thomas Carlyle's essay, "Biography," first published in *Fraser's Magazine* for April, 1832, twenty-seven years before Darwin's *Origin of Species*. The framework of stern Presbyterian asceticism in which Carlyle couches his thought about the meaning of a man's life which a biographer is to retail is filled with the elements which later implement the Darwinian vision. Every man is faced with a "Problem of Existence." The "struggle" of man against "material Necessity" is the very essence of "every man's Life." In this framework one has only to substitute for "every man's Life" the notion of the whole organic world, viewed as a unified organism of some sort struggling through the geological ages, and the Darwinian vision becomes a feasible thing. For in the Darwinian vision, the organic world is not a collection of various "natures" each born (*natura* originally means "birth") into a certain fixed level of perfection. Rather the entire organic world, and each item in it, is something more like the Christian soldier, the ascetic, striving to "make something" of itself, called on somehow to reach beyond its "natural" capacities to something higher. All the Christian vision is not caught in this Darwinian insight, but the conditioning of the insight by the Christian outlook is unmistakable.

IV

Other cases of interaction between religious and secular outlooks in the mind of modern man could be detailed. Particularly, one would like to go into the interaction between the personalist and "existential" philosophies which have grown up with the sense of history and of dialogue that marks our age, making this age quite as much the age of personalism and communication as it is the age of mechanization and technology—for personalist and mechanist developments stand in a dialectical or complementary relationship to one another. But enough has perhaps been said to lead to some reflections on religion, and particularly divine revelation, as related to secular disciplines. These reflections are concerned chiefly with the third of the periods which we have distinguished and in which we ourselves move, the age so dominated by a sense of history. I present the reflections from a Catholic point of view, but with the hope that they will be found not without interest and relevance for persons other than Catholics.

The sense of history with which contemporary thinkers all live has changed our entire basis for relating religion and the secular disciplines and has made apparent more than ever the need for relating them. The sense of history has eaten away at the idea of completely compartmentalized knowledges, for this idea fed on the conviction that individual arts and sciences were somehow complete a-temporal units, each capable of being "comprehended" in a kind of entirety once for all—as though, for example, one could know the field of geometry or physics in such a way as to have nothing more left to learn. Because we are now acutely aware that human knowledge comes into being in history and exists in history, we know that this is not so. Knowledges can expand indefinitely, and, as has been seen, their mode of expansion is often implemented in unexpected ways. A recent article in a professional chemical journal treats of the value of contemporary abstract or semi-abstract painting for furthering chemical discovery. Familiarity with such painting, which presents perceptions in novel and stimulating ways, may bring a chemist to view his own data and principles in fresh constellations and thus to advance his science.

To say that human knowledge comes into being in history is not at all the same as to say that human knowledge is "relative" in the sense that any statement is as true as any other, provided only that you wait long enough. At any given moment in history, men can discern certain truths and know that their contraries are certainly false. Rather, to say that human knowledge comes into being in history and exists in history is to say that it always specializes in one thing or another, one view or another, one outlook or another, and that its particular specialization is a correlative of its position in time. This is true even of the most abstract sciences. Mathematics has a history quite as much as biology or economics does. Of course, it is also to say that human knowledge in many ways progresses, and that its over-all pattern is cumulative. The store of knowledge carried in men's minds today is indubitably greater than that available to paleolithic or to neolithic man.

Now Christian revelation, too, comes into being in time. Jesus Christ is born into the world, suffers, dies, rises, and ascends to heaven as a "fulfillment of time." Our present intense awareness that human knowledge is a growing thing alerts us to the fact that God's intent was never to present the Gospel outside history. The Gospel was brought into the evolving, historical cosmos from the outside, yes, but in order to enter into this cosmos in its historical reality and, far from remaining outside that reality, to raise the historical process itself to God. There was a long pre-Mosaic historical preparation of the human race for the revelation of Himself which God gave the Hebrews. There was preparation in the organization of society, advanced from paleolithic to neolithic culture. There was preparation in the disciplines. It seems no accident that God waited until the alphabet had been invented and then gave His special revelation to one of the few peoples who had the alphabet. And His revelation becomes fuller and fuller with the history of the Hebrew nation, which itself is a revelation, a "type" or symbol of God's people in the New Testament, and which therefore must always be a part of the Christian consciousness. With the advent of Christ and the founding of His Church, formal revelation came to a close, in the sense that after the death of the last of the Apostles, according to Catholic teaching, no new public revelation was given to man. (Belief in private revelations, even to canonized saints, is by no means demanded of Catholics, and a sure sign of a bogus private revelation is its failure to conform to the public revelation made by Christ to His Church.) But the Church can, and most certainly does, reflect on the data of revelation and thus continually discovers new things in these data of which she had not been earlier aware, much in the way in which Copernicus reflected anew on the data of the astronomy of his time, and, *without the benefit of any new discoveries,* proposed an interpretation which tremendously advanced astronomy for his time and all times.

The Church, in Catholic teaching, is the organism in which

this reflective thinking and rethinking of revelation goes on—by means of individual endeavor, of course. The Church is Christ's Mystical Body, extending His Incarnation through all the history subsequent to His natural life on earth. Her teaching and thinking go on in history, extending the Incarnation within all the reality around her. Hence she has no choice about maintaining a close rapport with the secular disciplines, for these are an integral part of the world into which she protracts the Incarnation of Her Master. Her commitment to the secular disciplines was never greater than today. As formal schooling grows longer and longer to implement man's greater and greater intellectual, spiritual control over the brute matter in the universe, the various disciplines and their development become a more and more momentous part of human and cosmic history.

Since it is this developing world in which the various disciplines are playing a greater and greater role that the Church is called on to bring Christ, she has no choice about relating secular knowledge to theology. Thinkers in the Church must relate secular knowledges to theology and to her teaching, and this not merely to "reinterpret" her teaching for the age but also to possess it themselves in its fullness. For example, were theologians not to take advantage of the tremendous new insights into the meaning of person and personality developed through phenomenological and existentialist philosophy and through depth psychology, their very knowledge of Catholic doctrine concerning the Blessed Trinity, the Three Divine Persons in One Divine Nature, would exist at a subnormal level, below what is par for twentieth century thinking concerned with the question of person. Were theologians not to try to understand evolution, they would be failing to understand what the world, part of which Christ took to Himself as His own body, really is, and to this extent failing to understand as fully as they might the meaning of the Incarnation. Were they to fail to appreciate the technological age as an age which, like the age of the reptiles or the Pleistocene Epoch, forms a definite part of the mysterious evolution of the universe devised by God, they would be failing to develop decently the fuller meaning of the Incarnation as this can be developed today.

The Christian's stake, moreover, in the advance of secular knowledges is not merely negative. For, once the fact of evolution (of the cosmos, of life, and of our knowledge) is known, the Christian must recognize as God's work this upward movement in the universe, from brute matter to inorganic matter to man, and in human society from disjointed, less self-aware forms of social consciousness to a global awareness. For whose work other than God's could this development be? If this forward, upward movement is God's, the Christian has no choice but to try to further it. Thus the Church, with her theologians, must keep in touch with the whole universe-in-history, with its sciences and arts especially, in order to preach the Gospel to the whole world ("Catholic" means literally "through-the-whole"), to be present with Christ everywhere at the present front of history along which we ourselves live and which we are called on, under grace, to impregnate with Christ.

5
Research and American Catholic Education

Although the Church has been involved in education in one way or another from her very beginnings, and since the rise of the universities in the twelfth and thirteenth centuries has been involved in it with particular intensity, many very basic questions concerning education today under Catholic auspices have no fully thought-out answers. With Catholics, as with everyone else, the existential situation has preceded all explanation and always manages to keep ahead of it. In the large, explanation or theory can modify human activity, but it can never set it going. It will remain perpetually impossible fully to articulate the reasons why either the Church or any group of human beings is engaged in educational work.

Like other human activities, educational activity is antecedent to any rationalizations about it. Indeed, in any educational program, the chief operative reason why any given subject is taught or any procedure followed is usually, if somewhat less than always, not a theory at all but the simple fact that it was taught or followed before. Teachers are on hand with the necessary know-how. Because educational practice is concerned so largely with abstract ideas, we are likely to forget that it is like other human activities in that in great part it acts first and explains, even to itself, afterward.

The same is certainly true of many aspects of the Church's ventures in education. Educational work is an activity in which the Church has engaged for a multitude of reasons, some obvious, some obscure, some rationalized, others highly resistant to any formulation at all.

Perhaps more than other Catholics, American Catholics find this fact not easy to face. This is because they are Americans. The complications of the American psyche have frequently been pointed out. The American is the product of a past which is basically European but which has assimilated to itself other than European experiences. He is descended from persons who either abandoned their homes or were wrenched violently from them. He is in some sense subconsciously bewildered by the complexities of his own past. To simplify matters, to make them bearable, he tends to mythologize this past—and with it the present which is the living front of the past. One way to do this is to impute to the past itself what it did not have—resolution of the tensions and problems with which he himself has to wrestle. In this way, the confusing past out of which these problems arose becomes less terrifying. There was nothing wrong with it at all. His ancestors did not have to run away, knew no violence. The unsolved problems are only those in front of him. There are no dangers haunting him at the rear.

Somewhat in this fashion American Catholics are likely to feel their educational problems as simply extensions into the present of problems which the Church has faced for generations and knows intimately. Now some of our educational problems are of this sort, but many of them are not of this sort at all. Some of the most basic and most characteristic problems in American Catholic education, those concerned with the conduct of institutions of higher learning—colleges and universities—are new and quite unsolved.

First of all, the formal educational program directly sponsored by the Church in the present-day United States involves the education of a much more mature and advanced group of persons than earlier Church-sponsored educational programs or than most Church-sponsored educational programs elsewhere today. American Catholic universities and colleges represent a direct large-scale venture into higher education such as the Catholic Church has never attempted in the past or elsewhere in the present. The first universities, those of medieval Europe, were certainly the product of a Catholic society and of a Catholic frame of mind, but they were not institutions formed by priests or ecclesiastics under the direct administration of priests or ecclesiastics. The masters of arts, not the masters of theology, administered the University of Paris, and masters of arts were more likely to be aligned with the medical than with the theological faculty. Through papal bulls the university secured certain international privileges, but it was not founded by directive of the Pope or of any other bishop, nor were the universities at Oxford or Cambridge or at Bologna or Salamanca.

In Renaissance times universities did come into being under more direct ecclesiastical sponsorship both in Catholic and in Protestant countries. But these were seldom large-scale operations in higher education. As Father George E. Ganss's excellent work, *Saint Ignatius' Idea of a Jesuit University*, has shown, most early Jesuit universities consisted in actuality of what would today be a secondary school (a very good one, with an intensive curriculum) and a faculty of theology which taught practically no one but students for the priesthood who themselves commonly finished theology around the age of twenty, younger and less mature than many of our present undergraduates. In a similar tradition, the arts course, including all of philosophy, at medieval universities could be finished and the degree of master of arts acquired when a boy was only eighteen—except at Paris, where more stringent statutes demanded that a master of arts be at least twenty.

Secondly, at the college and university level, education is much more a liberal education in the United States than elsewhere. Most Americans, Catholic or other, are rather uniformly startled when this fact is pointed out to them. They believe that European universities are more humanistically or liberally oriented than American—and this largely because they want to believe so. Perhaps nothing illustrates the tendency of Americans to mythologize their past, and the country of their past, which even today is Europe, according to their own needs than this curious and widespread belief about European higher education. Campaigns to develop liberal education, typically American phenomena, are thus rationalized and indued with force and conviction. The father-image is made over into a picture of what one wants oneself to be.

As a matter of fact, European higher education, on the Continent and in the British Isles, is rather uniformly specialized, and even secondary education, preparatory for higher education, is more specialized than Europeans can admit without discomfort. In the Netherlands or Germany or France or Italy or England, when a student goes to the university he goes there to specialize, even in his undergraduate work—in mathematics or in physics or in economics or in the classical languages or in philosophy or sometimes in a special combination of such items. The undergraduate doing mathematics at Oxford or Leyden or Paris studies nothing but mathematics—no history, no literature, nothing else. European universities today still generally preserve the theoretically professional orientation of the medieval universities. Liberal education is provided—supposedly in its entirety—in the secondary schools, which, to be sure, do keep the student until he is generally about a year older than he would be at the end of American secondary schooling. These secondary schools, which provide this liberal education, were dissociated from the universities at the time of the Renaissance, when their aims became vastly different from those of the universities, and they have remained dissociated ever since. Such schools constitute the Renaissance and post-Renaissance "colleges"—*collèges, colegios, Kollegien, collegia,* in the sense in which this term occurs in most educational documents until quite recent years. We have had such "colleges" in the United States, but, beginning with Harvard College, they have tended to grow up into universities, thus establishing inside the American university certain nonprofessional, liberal attitudes typical of the Renaissance humanists' outlook rather than of the standard European university tradition. In this milieu, what was more natural than that the original Catholic "colleges" conceived of in the United States at first according to Old World models as humanistic secondary schools, should follow suit and grow into universities themselves—institutions more variegated and more integrated in the bourgeois society around them than European universities have ever been? This fascinating evolution of our old Catholic "colleges" into present-day American colleges and universities should be kept in mind in any discussion of scholarly research by members of our faculties, if only for the reason that it may militate sometimes against scholarly research. Because of their history, American Catholic colleges and universities may tend to feel to some of their faculty members as merely extensions of high school. This tendency is less marked now than formerly, but it was a very real tendency only a few decades ago. It has had its parallel in American Protestant and secular educational circles.

The relative maturity of our college and university students and the existence of some kind of ambition to impart a humanistic or liberal education to those students, or at least to those of them in the colleges of arts and sciences and often enough in some vague way to others, too, has introduced into the American curriculum patterns which were quite unheard of in earlier education. Until very recent times, for example, literature was a subject with which students commonly terminated their classroom contact at about the age of fourteen. Practically speaking, literature was cultivated less for what we should today call "appreciation" than as a means of familiarizing a boy with Latin so that he could read and speak and write it fluently enough to get along in the learned or professional world. We must not forget that everywhere in Western Europe and America until not much more than a hundred years ago the study of literature meant commonly the study of Latin literature only, with a dash of Greek. The vernacular was not taught as a regular school subject, except to very tiny boys when they were learning to write and perhaps to identify the parts of speech. But it was frequently prescribed that a boy be able to do these things before he was admitted to a regular school. This Latin-centered education was accepted in Protestant and Catholic environments alike.

Because of our own complex history a myth has been generated in the minds of American Catholics which imputes to earlier Catholic educators attitudes toward literature which few of them had, and which the curriculum had hardly at all. Father Martin Antonio Delrio, S.J., famous for his book on magic and witchcraft and for many other books, in the Preface to his edition of Seneca's plays, *Syntagma tragoediae*

Latinae (Antwerp, 1614), is quite outspoken in stating the common view that the "lowly humane letters" (*humiliores et humaniores litterae*) are for little boys, to toughen them for the weightier disciplines of philosophy, medicine, law, and theology, and that the only concern adults should manifest with poetry, drama, and literature generally is to undertake to edit it for the use of little boys or to teach it to them. Despite all his Stoicism, Seneca might have been just a little shaken to hear this from his editor. But the fact is that in Father Delrio's world, generally speaking (there were some exceptions), we find no course in literature for boys at the level of juniors or seniors in high school, much less at college level, not to mention the graduate school level. Philosophy was not much better off, since formal courses in it terminated —as they terminate in European schools today for all those who do not specialize in philosophy at the university—around the age of seventeen, or even sixteen.

To get a better view of the novelty of the situations with which we are faced today and which we take for granted as age-old, it is well to recall also that in the Constitutions of the Society of Jesus and in the early *Ratio studiorum,* or *Method of Studies,* which governed Jesuit educational procedure, the only textbook mentioned for formal courses in religion—other than strictly professional courses in theology —is the catechism. When a boy knew his catechism, his formal religious education was complete—although the Sodality and other means were available for his growth in personal holiness and apostolic activity. In the past generation Catholic educators all over the world have been undertaking the truly revolutionary work of devising textbooks which can be used for regular secondary-school courses in religion, and in the United States—almost alone—an effort is being made to work out satisfactory courses in religion or theology at the college and university level for students other than those studying for the priesthood. In the highly specialized European university, to this day the pattern is different. A person doing an undergraduate degree, for example, in mathematics might be intensely interested in religion and, as at the Centre Richelieu at the University of Paris, attend extracurricular lectures on the Catholic faith. But he would no more think of enrolling for a university course in theology or "religion" than a medical student would in an American university. We are obviously living in an intellectual world of a different shape from that of two hundred years ago and even from that of the present day outside the United States.

A third factor may be mentioned as productive of new problems, a factor in many ways more radical than the age of the students we deal with or the liberal bent of the educational setting in which we operate. This factor is the condition of the entire intellectual enterprise of mankind since the discovery of evolution. By evolution here I mean not only cosmic evolution and the evolution of species, but the evolution of thought itself. The perspectives in time and space opened by the geological and anthropological sciences, and the awareness of the profundities of history which has come with the same perspectives, have made man acutely aware of the fact that all thought, including the most abstract scientific thought, is a growing thing. With our improved penetration of the past, the remoteness of the intellectual world of even St. Thomas Aquinas, not to mention Aristotle, from our own has become distressingly evident.

This is not to say that we cannot at all follow the thinking of men in the past, or that we cannot learn something from them. Quite the contrary: we *must* study them. But it is to say that to get back into the routes of their thinking is a laborious business. To find what St. Thomas means by *intentio* or what Aristotle means by *hypostasis* involves a tremendous amount of work, of back-tracking through the labyrinths of intellectual history. We know that we can never recapture the totality of St. Thomas' view of the universe, even if we wanted to, if only because we cannot forget enough of what man has thought and discovered since his time. Extrapolating in the other direction, with vistas of human intellectual developments reaching ahead of us for tens and hundreds of thousands of years, we see that "following" St. Thomas, or anyone else, can hardly mean quite what "following" a teacher meant when the world was thought to have been created in 4004 B.C. and to have a life expectancy proportioned to this modest, and totally inadequate, figure. We have only to take thought to be aware that the science of physics, let us say, fifty thousand years from now—or even the science of geometry—will exist in a condition which we at present could hardly recognize. These sciences will doubtless encompass what we now know in their fields, as modern geometry encompasses Euclidean together with a great many other geometries, but the dialogue in which all human knowledge is held will have advanced so far that the very terms in which it is carried on even a few generations from now, and much more fifty thousand years from now, will involve concepts which we have never yet learned to form. This shows the living developmental character of all human knowledge, for the differences detectable over a range of several thousand years are only the increment of day-by-day differences.

An intense consciousness of this developmental pattern in human knowledge is today part of the standard equipment of every moderately well-educated man. It has led not only to the historical outlook now taken for granted in the better studies of medieval scholastic philosophy and of all philosophy, but to Einstein's feeling that even the formulae of theoretical physics had to be complemented with a detailed account of the developmental process itself whereby these formulae were evolved, such as we find in the book Einstein wrote with Leopold Infeld, *The Evolution of Physics*.

The enlargement of our perspectives regarding the development of human knowledge in time has been accompanied by a corresponding enlargement of perspective regarding its development in space. We are becoming daily more and more aware not only of the similarity of various human cultures scattered over the face of the globe but also of their divergencies. Our understanding of the Scriptures has been revolutionized by the study of Semitic culture and its differences from Western European culture. And what must the effect be of our attitude toward such a basic subject as grammar when we realize the fact that whole far-advanced civilizations have done entirely without it, and that to this day the Chinese never teach a grammar of their language in school as a matter of principle—not only because grammar is less possible in Chinese than in English but also because, as they will tell you, to erect and enforce a grammar of Chinese would kill the language by stifling its normal development and making it less effective as a means of communication? (This condition may well change with the introduction of the Roman alphabet to replace character writing now going forward in China—grammar is profoundly oriented toward an alphabetic culture, for it is in a special sense the study of "letters," in Greek *grammata*.)

It has, of course, been as true in the past as in the present that human knowledge was a divergent and growing thing. But by the present time, having grown through history in the reflectiveness and self-consciousness peculiar to spiritual beings, we have come to an awareness of this aspect of knowledge more intense and urgent than ever before. It is true that in the past within the Church, at least in certain countries or among certain groups of persons, there has been a strong tradition of scholarly research and publication such as might entail some sense of knowledge as a growing thing. However, today the need to develop this tradition further has become more and more apparent, particularly in the United States. The chief reasons seem to be those just suggested. First, the Church has never been so directly in the work of higher education at all to the extent to which she is in this work in the United States today. Secondly, studies which in an earlier era were purveyed regularly only at a lower curricular level—such as literature or philosophy, not to mention theology—are now purveyed at a much higher level in our colleges and universities. Thirdly, we live in a society acutely aware that human knowledge is a growing knowledge.

II

This third fact is the most important, for it means that an adequate induction into knowledge, an induction which will inspire students and remain as a viable part of their intellectual possessions, must be one in which knowledge is communicated to them as a growing thing, with promise of still greater growth. In a world which, consciously and subconsciously, knows as much about development as ours does, real interest in a subject has become inseparable from interest in the further development of the subject. This applies to college and university education generally; but it applies the more urgently the higher one moves in the curriculum and the more capable the student in question. And who can say how many students judged incapable are so precisely because they have never had an instructor who could communicate this sense of living and growing knowledge? I myself feel convinced that at the upper-division college level it has become quite impossible to communicate a subject in any viable fashion without communicating at least some sort of feeling for the growth of the field being taught. Radically, all human knowledge is held in a dialogue setting. The most abstruse mathematical theorem is, in the last analysis, something that some individual *says* to others. To pretend that it is otherwise, that knowledge lies in the mind not as a germ or growing thing which was started with the help of other persons and with which one has to work all one's life always in terms destined of their very nature to be communicated to others, but that it lies in the mind as an inert mass picked up from somewhere outside human society, is not only to court pedagogical failure but to play false with truth itself.

This condition of knowledge as a growing thing is the ultimate basis for the absolute need for research and publication in our colleges and universities. Development, which comes from research, is not a frosting on the cake of human knowledge. It never was, although men may have implied or even said so in the past—Francisco de Vitoria, the sixteenth century theologian, states that there are no new discoveries possible in physics—and now it cannot even be made to appear to be. Research is of the very stuff of human knowledge. If you do not work on the knowledge you have, it will work on you—will generate from within your own prejudices and presuppositions all sorts of bogus conclusions, implied or at times stated outright. Because medieval and Renaissance theologians had not worked out in enough detail the relations of cosmology and revealed truth, there was generated in their minds, without their being aware of it, a quite false notion of this relationship, terminating in the ill-starred Galileo decision. The tragedy is that some illusion that knowledge is static can be maintained today by restricting one's contacts to pupils, and to pupils who have a very elementary outlook—that is, to those who by definition are not as yet in touch with the reality of the situation and hence cannot feel the growth of knowledge as a mature scholar can. This, I am afraid, is what we all do if we do not keep up with the research in our fields. And thus restricting one's contacts is possible only at the sacrifice of the pupils' own minds, only by a terrible kind of injustice on the part of the teacher, who thus deforms those most sacredly charged to his care—and, what is worst, most deforms those who have the greatest possibilities.

Our present awareness of the essentially growing nature of human knowledge poses certain special problems for the clerical mind everywhere, but these problems are being brought very rapidly to a head in the United States. If there has been in the past a "clerical mind," such a mind turned to research would seem to have been more given to compilation than to original discovery. Copernicus was a cleric, it appears, if not an ordained priest, and Gregor Mendel an Augustinian monk, but for every Copernicus and Mendel there has been a seeming infinity of intellectual retailers among clerics, from medieval manuscript copyists to Johann Eck, compiler of theological "places" or loci (whence one could "draw out" arguments against Protestantism), or Father Jasper Heywood, who contributed to the great era of English drama, certainly, but by translating Seneca, not by writing anything very original of his own.

It might be argued that the incidence of creativity among clerics is quite as high as it has been in the past among physicians, lawyers, physical scientists, and teachers generally. This may be so. The question is not so much the high or low incidence of creativity as the respect shown for it and the desire enkindled to develop it. The dominantly defensive study of theology for the past three or four centuries has done anything but encourage original thinking and discovery, and theology is a powerful force in fixing the habits of the clerical mind. At present theology, particularly in scriptural studies, is showing some signs of a change. But the clerical mind is not yet a symbol of venturesome discovery. It symbolizes rather order, which, in this erratic sublunary world, often supervenes only long after discovery is finished with.

In the United States today the field of higher learning and education is being peopled more and more by clerics—both in the strict sense of those in holy orders and in the wide sense which would include also members of religious institutes of men not in holy orders (lay brothers) and of women (sisters). The pressure is building up to develop among this entire group devotion to discovery, and with it a more intense awareness of the inevitable fact that intellectual discovery is of itself a spiritual good and hence of itself work for God's cause. The effects of this growing devotion and awareness remain to be seen, both on the clerical mind generally and upon the types of person who in the future will be attracted to the clerical life. We may, with some reason, look for rather more John Henry Newmans and fewer Dr. Cullens.

III

But, whatever the present awareness of the expanding nature of human knowledge and whatever the effects of this awareness on Catholic clergy and laity, do those engaged in Catholic educational work have to do research themselves? Can we not just keep up with that done by others? Speaking generally, I am most profoundly convinced that a school, a faculty, a department and, as far as possible, the individuals in the department need to do research themselves. For if knowledge is set in a dialogue and moving forward in a dialogue setting, it is by taking part in the dialogue that we learn. A bystander is too uninterested, too uncommitted. And if there is anything that our American Catholic education suffers from, it is the fact that too many of us are not committed to the subjects we profess, not dedicated to them with that total dedication which, for us, should be part of our religious dedication to God Himself, Who makes human knowledge to advance. By commitment I mean dedication of the sort which makes us genuinely afflicted, makes us sad, when fields we are interested in—biology or law or medicine or government or mathematics—make little progress and makes us happy and enthusiastic when we see the results of original and profound thinking in our fields. There is no way to dedicate oneself to learning from the outside. One's dedication is from within the subject. And this dedication for us lies itself not outside, but inside, one's own vocation, religious or lay.

The clergy and religious have special difficulties, as well as special opportunities, here. In my limited experience, the one thing which lay teachers detect all too often in priests and religious is a horrible insouciance, not about their students as persons, but about the subject into which they are most solemnly charged to induct these pupils. There is, I believe, no way to be a real college or university teacher while remaining exterior to one's subject and uncommitted to its propagation and development. Because of his or her special personal dedication to God, the priest or religious can manage a total dedication to a field of learning which is perhaps more difficult, other things being equal, for the layman to achieve. But if the priest or religious fails here, his failure is more of a scandal.

Since the intellectual universe, like the physical universe, is a developing one, and since creation and its activity, sin excepted, is God's work, as Catholics we should be more interested than non-Catholics in furthering intellectual development. For to further it is to intensify the spiritual component in the universe, and thus to open new frontiers for the free working of grace. It is true, of course, that increase in knowledge is a risk: it opens new possibilities for evil as well as for good. But the very existence of a spiritual being, man, in the universe has involved a terrible risk. For all but the last few hundred thousand years of its five to ten billion years of existence, the universe was free from sin for the simple reason that, so far as we know, there was no person in it to do any sinning. Yet Almighty God colonized it with mankind, let man spread over the face of the earth, impregnating the impersonal mass of the cosmos with intellect and will in the persons of men. This was a risk, a calculated risk, we might say, on God's part. This introduction of the spiritual, the free component, into His material creation made moral evil possible. Yet it opened an avenue to grace in the mass of brute matter which was the cosmos. God took this risk, and He increases it daily as He brings man into a position of greater dominance over the forces of brute matter.

For, although such increase, or any increment in the intellectual or spiritual component in the universe, is a further risk, it increases the field of operation for grace itself. Grace moves where God wills, and yet it does not move the sea or the mountain or even the ape. The Holy Spirit moves where He will, and yet we note that public revelation on a major scale, the revelation given to Abraham and his descendants, waited a long time—most likely some four hundred thousand or more years after man's first appearance on earth —until the intellectual achievement of the alphabet, this strange device invented only once in the history of mankind, and then it was given to one of the peoples who had the alphabet. How could public revelation have been passed on in a paleolithic age, or even in most neolithic ages, when men were scattered over the earth for tens or hundreds of thousands of years in tiny isolated clusters unable to enter into effective communication with one another and even ignorant of one another's existence? Theology is becoming increasingly aware of the development of revelation not only "from above," through communication from God, but also "from below," through the preparation of the cosmos and of human society and of the intellectual equipment of the human consciousness itself for the effective reception of revelation and the continuous penetrating of its meaning. The development of man's intellect is certainly part of this preparation, and this development, we now know, is spread out not only through the life of the individual but through the collective life of the human race. Such development, whatever risk it entails, is necessarily God's work. For it seems that God's work is always, from our point of view, a risk.

IV

If it is true that the intellectual universe is a developing one and that its development is God's work and hence something which can claim the allegiance of Catholics even more than that of non-Catholics, what are some of the pressing needs in this development felt by American Catholic education today? I cannot hope to rehearse them all, but it may be of some service to indicate those which seem to me to be the most pressing.

There is first the need for research in theology, for theology, above all, is a science which cannot afford to stand still. Mixing God's revealed word with misunderstanding is horribly disastrous, and we are pretty sure so to mix it if we do not keep this knowledge in constant contact with theology. Otherwise new questions arise which cannot be understood in old frames of reference, and which, being misunderstood, are provided with incorrect answers. The theological frames of reference have to keep pace with other thinking, and even, if possible, get ahead of other thinking. What might the results have been if, at the time of the lamentable Galileo decision, theology had been developed to the point where it could have provided an adequate understanding of the relationship of divine revelation to the physical sciences, at least such understanding as exists today, and if linguistic and cultural studies had only been further developed themselves and laid hold of by theologians to interpret Josue x 12? We should not have the unfortunate facts on the historical record that until 1757 all books which said that the earth went around the sun were *ipso facto* on the *Index of Forbidden Books,* that Catholic schools could not, at least until this date and in practice often did not until long after this date, teach that the earth went around the sun, that as late as the year 1820 a book so stating was refused the imprimatur in Rome, and that only in 1822 was the general permission to print such books in Rome finally granted.

The development of theology has become an urgent, and even desperate, one in American Catholic colleges and universities where mature students are constantly dealing with and themselves developing questions crying for theological answers or commentary which the theology taught in seminary courses does not provide. There is a need here for what we might call a "university theology" to complement the post-Tridentine seminary theology, with its strongly pastoral and apologetic bent. The strength of this seminary theology lies in great part in its conservatism, but it is simply not enough to be conservative if we wish to Christianize a universe which we now know is in active evolution. If we have to bring our university students—even undergraduates, but much more graduate students—to take part in the forward movement of thought, as we do, then we have to provide them with a theology which is participating in this forward movement, for this forward movement itself must be Christianized, impregnated with grace.

The irony of our theological situation has become critical, and it consists in this. Here in the United States we have the largest and most effective venture which the Church as such has ever made in higher education—far larger, far more effective, and far more explicitly Christian than that in the Middle Ages, when the huge faculty of arts, not the relatively tiny faculty of theology, commonly provided the rectors of universities such as Paris. Yet, despite the fact that we have for the first time in Christian history a huge network of universities directed by theologically trained men, we have no major theology faculty at any university with the exception of that at Catholic University, which has, understandably, a strong pastoral bent, and, alone, can hardly make its principal concern the burning intellectual problems of the *university* milieu.

We must face the fact that today where original theological work is being done by Catholic theologians, it is where the theological faculty is part of a university—as at Innsbruck or Strasbourg or Louvain—operating and thinking at the intellectual fronts which a university keeps open, or where the theological faculty is inside a city which is a major university center—such as at Paris or Lyons or, until recently, at Zikawei in China—and in which contact with the intellectual front is not only inevitable but assiduously cultivated. In the United States we have failed to bring our theology into vital contact with our own university milieus, isolating our theology faculties from the university campus, with the result that even a place such as Austria, with a total population of some seven million, by no means all of them practicing Catholics, has been incomparably more productive theologically than we. We are also faced with the curious fact that no university offers a theological course open to women. Undoubtedly many others have had the same experience as I when I was approached by a brilliant young Catholic woman with the complaint, "I can go to any university to get a degree in any other subject I wish if I can master the material [she already has her doctorate in one subject], but when I apply to a Catholic university for a course leading toward a theological degree, I am told that this is not a fit subject for women!"

Something similar obtains in philosophy, where the real problems raised in the minds of the most active and promising students are all too often scanted or avoided in favor of other problems which it has become simply customary to treat. The need for research and publication here is, I dare say, the greatest perhaps in cosmology. Although it might be argued that working out a cosmology of the world as we really know it is primarily a theological task, that a Christology of the post-Darwinian and post-Einsteinian universe is our basic need here, nevertheless there is the problem of a contemporary philosophical cosmology to be faced. Such a cosmology cannot come into existence so long as we think of the enterprise of constructing it as a process of catching up with the scientific front, of shooting down so-called difficulties lobbed back from this front (which we have manwhile never even visited), or as a process of retouching old medieval cosmologies.

A viable and meaningful cosmology must be the work of those somehow at the scientific front themselves, pushing it ahead, sharing its enthusiasms and its visions. It is significant that the one Catholic cosmology which has caught the imaginations of thinking men, won their admiration, and sometimes won them to the Church, has been the cosmology —call it theological or philosophical as you will, for it is both—generated in the mind of a man who was at the forefront of anthropological discovery, Père Pierre Teilhard de Chardin, who was one of the co-discoverers of the Peking Man. For the effect in strictly scientific circles of a Jesuit completely devoted to his God, to the Church, and to the Order to which he belonged, and at the same time sincerely committed to the advance of science as God's work, one can refer to the wonderful tributes to Père Teilhard in *Science* for January, 1956, and the *American Anthropologist* for February, 1956. The former concludes with the statement by Professor Hallam L. Movius, Jr., of the Peabody Museum at Harvard University, that the spiritual "was as vital to him as the purely physical evidence, and in his ability to sustain and teach this belief he was head and shoulders above those of us who are left here to carry on the work." If we are going to hold our best university products for Christ, to inspire them to give themselves to Him and to His Father, we are going to have to provide them with the same sense of challenge in cosmology and the rest of philosophy which they are meeting in the best courses they get from other departments in the university.

The need for research, of a peculiarly perceptive and active type, is just as great in literature as in philosophy. Literature requires scholarship, firsthand working with sources, and their constant reworking, for in literature, above all, we have an active and moving front. Our knowledge of literary history makes it impossible to teach the epic or Shakespearean drama or the novel as static moments in the past, or to appreciate their beauties in terms of such moments. We know that there was a time when there were no epics, in the classical and postclassical sense of this term, and a time when there was no drama of the Shakespearean sort, and a time, not very long ago, when there was no novel. Literature and literary forms are a part of the mysterious pattern of cosmic evolution planned by Almighty God and must be evaluated with some appreciation of this pattern. Literary species, or genres, like biological species, arise and disappear, and in doing so give rise to new species. In this setting we do not even know what to teach unless we keep ourselves intimately aware of the pattern of development, for the study of literature here becomes the study of a growing thing in which, as T. S. Eliot has pointed out in his capital essay "Tradition and the Individual Talent," the past is not only forming and giving meaning to new works but the new works themselves are altering and enlarging and deepening the meaning of the past.

Thus it becomes imperative that all literature—even ancient literature—be taught by persons who are aware not only of scholarly developments in their fields, but also of developments in contemporary literature, felt and known intimately as the wave front of a long past. In W. B. Stanford's work, *The Ulysses Theme,* which traces this theme from Homer and before down to the present day, the fuller meaning of Homer's Odysseus becomes more evident from our knowledge of the Ulysses of James Joyce and the still more recent Ulysses of Nikos Kazantzakis. An interpretation of Ulysses or of any other item from past literature which works from no familiarity with contemporary literary developments is at best a half-interpretation. For it approaches past literature out of the twentieth century without really understanding the twentieth century. It seeks to interpret literature for present-day man without taking into account the literary activity of present-day literary men. It is thus basically an illiterate presentation of literature. Of course, the converse is true: contemporary literature can be mastered only with some knowledge of its past.

Time was when it was possible and common in Catholic and all other schools as well to look on literature in the classroom as primarily and directly a means of inculcating morals. This view of literature is a very ancient one, Platonic and older, and it was encouraged in earlier schools by what we have seen to be the extreme youth of the pupils studying literature and the consequent need to strain literature of anything but the most simple and obvious kind of "message," as well as by the absence of courses in religion after the catechism, with the consequent inclination to make other courses substitute and give depth to catechetical lessons. This may be all right when literature is taught up to the age of fourteen years and no further. It will not do for intelligent undergraduates at the lower-division level, much less at the upper-division level, and still less at the graduate level. Literature is not independent of morals any more than life is, but it is not written normally simply to teach a thesis in ethics. It is written for reasons far more complicated than that and in the long run quite awesome. If we are going to get from it anything satisfying to the mature mind, we are going to have to approach literature in a humble spirit of appreciation and inquiry, as a manifestation, and an exceedingly complex and mysterious one, of man's relationship to the reality around him. This will permit no cavalier attitudes. It demands research and continuous revision of research.

As a fourth and last sample for illustration—for I cannot attempt to review all the subjects even in the college of arts and sciences, much less those in all areas of instruction—we can take the social sciences. Here the disasters attendant upon a lack of research and publication by Catholic scholars is all too evident in the past. In the past we find that, as a result of not having active Catholic scholars at the intellectual front in institutions of higher learning, the sociological revolution in human society had almost passed by before the Catholic consciousness became aware of it. We make much, and rightly, of the papal encyclicals on social justice. But, to tell the truth, Catholic documents on social justice were slow in coming and were at first very few. And they were still slower in being felt. The failure and mistakes of Catholics which lost the nineteenth century urban immigration in Europe to the Church was in great part a failure in research and scholarship—in not being at the forefront of the thinking of the age. The great spate of intellectual activity which heralded the present-day interest in the social sciences and the founding of socialist parties and which was marked by the presence of Saint-Simon, Robert Owen, Fourier, Comte, and John Stuart Mill was a phenomenon well under way a century and a half ago. Saint-Simon was born in 1760, and the year 1957 marked the hundredth anniversary of Comte's death. If the Church in the eighteenth and nineteenth centuries had had a group of men at the forefront of the intellectual movements of the time, taking part in and spurring on in a Christian context this great, if often erratic, development of thought, how different would be the fate of the urbanized workers in Continental Europe, where the very existence of changed social conditions was not recognized generally by the Catholic conscience until whole generations too late! But the intellectual life of the Church in the eighteenth and nineteenth centuries was at an unfortunately low ebb.

We are doing somewhat better today—two centuries after the birth of the men whose work marked the orientation of Western thinking toward the social problem—but even today a recent book reviewing the contribution of Catholic thinkers to sociological thought is all too evidently a brave attempt to make the most of relatively scant evidence. What is significant here is not that we do not teach the social sciences. We teach them—perhaps even too many and too much of them. But we teach them all too often as something we have stumbled upon or borrowed or even found forced upon us, not as something we have made our own by passionate intellectual commitment and sacrifices. Sometimes, alas, it is even worse: we have been schooled to resent these studies, and many others, as intruders in what was supposedly an orderly universe before their advent.

In this brief and inadequate treatment of the necessity of

research and publication in American Catholic colleges and universities I have passed over the natural sciences. My warrant for this is the fact that in these sciences the need is the most obvious of all from the point of view which I consider most basic and which I have sought to develop here, that is, from the point of view that knowledge is something which must be continually advancing if it is to be anything at all. We have enough television sets and other mechanical marvels as obvious, and sometimes noisy, by-products to make it perfectly evident that the natural sciences are advancing. Everyone knows, or can well imagine, that physics fifty thousand years from now will be something projected far beyond what physics is today, will include today's physics, but in modes of conceptualization so enlarged and elaborated and, no doubt, in many ways so simplified that we should not be able to enter into a knowledge of this physics of the future without passing somehow through the historical development which will have intervened between physicists of that day and physicists of our time. And so with chemistry, with medicine, and other such subjects.

What I hope to have brought home here is that this condition of continuous growth, simplification, recapitulation, and irresistible *élan* obtains in all human knowledge—not only in physics and in chemistry and medicine and the other natural sciences, but also, in a different but equally real way, in the study of literature and philosophy and theology, too. We have only to think of the knowledge of literary forms and their history, or of the state of philology and linguistics in Cicero's day or St. Isidore of Seville's day as compared to our own, or of the discussion concerning existence itself in Aristotle's day or St. Thomas' as compared to our own (M. Gilson, not St. Thomas, is the one who has made a point of the existentialism in St. Thomas' writings), or of the condition of Scriptural study in the time of St. Jerome as compared to our own time, to sense how development is built into our process of knowing in these areas, too.

V

In this chapter I have, I am aware, said nothing of practicalities such as teaching loads, departmental organization, administrative needs, financial problems, and the like. These are administrative problems to be solved, and I am inexperienced and probably incompetent as an administrator. But they must be felt as problems in the proper context, which for a college or university is necessarily that of teaching—and, by this very fact, necessarily that of research and publication. Administrators, too—indeed, administrators especially—must have a vision of what the stuff of education consists in, of *what sort of thing it is*. Not only is the educational process complicated in terms of the persons involved, but the subject "matter" itself is not a capsule in the minds of those who teach it, nor can it become such in the minds of those who really learn it. For administrators to suppose, even subconsciously, that it is a capsule rather than a growing germ, vitiates and makes ineffectual the whole process of higher education. Our vision of knowledge must make it clear that that is not what knowledge is.

What I have tried to say is, then, in summary, that new discovery, and the publication which goes with it and which is the sharing of this new discovery with others in the world in which we have learned to make the discovery, is not something superadded to the process of knowing and learning and teaching. It is integral—indeed, central—to these processes themselves. When a college or university faculty is out of touch with research to the extent that its members are making no contribution to research at all, who is going to be in touch with research? Such a faculty cannot avoid in some sort deforming the mind of its students when it should be forming them. It cannot help being false to its most sacred obligation, which urges itself upon Catholics with particular force, the obligation to help men to know.

The obligation which the Church has taken up in her educational enterprises presents to all Catholics always an inspiring challenge. But today in the United States at the college and university level it is more of a challenge than ever before. If what I have said here by way of appraisal is outspoken, it is so because Catholic education in this country has behind it a solid enough achievement to enable it to be outspoken in its self-criticism without danger of suffering from discouragement, and because we feel that opportunity to develop in research and publication is a more real opportunity today than at any time hitherto in this land. If we feel acutely, and even desperately, the need for Catholics really competent in their fields and devoted wholeheartedly to intellectual activity, the growth in the number of Catholics lay and clerical meeting these requirements is notable. But we must never forget that we are faced with an opportunity so great that we have hardly even begun to do it justice. In particular, the opportunity to develop what I have called a "university theology," a theology of original research and publication in intimate touch with the most active intellectual fields in our time, is one greater than the Church has ever known anywhere in her past history. The chief reason for being outspoken in our self-appraisal is this: the need to know the *real* place in history of our educational activity, to know the past in the real present and the present in the real past, so that Catholics can see the work which God has willed that we undertake as the stimulating challenge to creativity that it is.

6
The Apostolate of Secular Arts and Sciences

The development of the Church's interest in higher education in the United States has raised questions concerning the relationship of the secular and the sacred more urgent than ever before. Since the beginnings of Christianity, and before, such questions have, of course, been frequently agitated, and the agitation has left in its wake various expressions and formulae which still bob about in discussion today: theology as the queen of the sciences, philosophy as the handmaid of theology, morning knowledge and evening knowledge, subordination and subalternation of sciences to one another, the doctrine of the two swords, and so on. But none of these expressions or formulae quite engages the reality of the secular-sacred relationship as this exists in Catholic higher educational circles today.

The problem here today is less centered than before on the abstract relationship of theological knowledge to knowledge, for example, in the natural sciences or to mathematics or to depth psychology. Rather it concerns the relationship between the commitment of the Church, the Mystical Body of Christ, to revealed religion on the one hand and on the other her commitment, or lack of commitment, to secular knowledge. Earlier in history, and even today in most places outside the United States, this particular question could hardly arise. Universities grew up within Christendom, and like many institutions in medieval society, they sought and found some sort of ecclesiastical backing and approval. But they were not ecclesiastical foundations in the way in which American Catholic universities and colleges are.

From the Renaissance on, it is true that "colleges" were founded by specifically religious bodies, Catholic and Protestant, but these colleges were in intent and in actuality close to our secondary schools, not our universities. The universities which came into existence in post-Renaissance Europe as specifically religious foundations were few indeed, and were either so specialized (as the Gregorian University, which is a theological and philosophical educational institution all but entirely for clerics) or so small or short-lived that they did not pose the kind of problem posed in the United States today. Occasionally present-day Catholic foundations outside the United States, such as at Beirut or Milan or Bogotá, do pose the same kind of problem, as the National University has in Ireland, where Newman's lectures published as *The Idea of a University* formulated some of the issues. But because these are all individual and more or less isolated institutions, they do not pose the problems with the same massive urgency as do the 259 Catholic institutions of higher learning in the United States.

In brief, the framework of the problem posed by these Catholic institutions of higher learning is the following. In the United States the Church herself, acting through her regularly constituted hierarchical channels, has actually—if, as we shall see, in a sense indirectly—set up or founded universities and university-level colleges. She has been able to do this because of a pattern rather peculiar to American life whereby colleges and universities, Catholic or not, throughout the country are normally controlled in great part by a board of trustees or some similar group separate from the teaching staff. This staff is simply made up of persons which the board or its equivalent secures to do the teaching, generally by hiring on the open market. This arrangement has been the subject of recent comment, and of some complaint, on the part of Professor Howard Mumford Jones and others. But it remains a fact in the United States. Universities are founded and more or less controlled by groups who do not have the same commitments to learning which the persons who actually constitute the core of the university—the teaching faculty—themselves have. This arrangement obtains not only in Catholic but in other American universities and colleges as well, religiously sponsored and secular.

It is true that outside the United States something of this condition exists wherever governments have founded universities, as they certainly have done. For the government is indubitably an extra-academic entity which in some sense recruits an academic faculty. But in the European tradition at least, government-founded universities come into being in a historical setting in which the original universities were not government foundations at all, although they may have been government-aided. The present government-founded University of Paris is the successor of a medieval university whose "faculties" (in the European sense, both teachers and students taken jointly) were not even subject to civil law. Hence, in this setting, one often finds insistence on the "autonomy" of universities written into university statutes explicitly, and a general acknowledgment that universities are communities of scholars left pretty much to manage their own business. The right of having their own representatives

The Apostolate of Secular Arts and Sciences

in Parliament enjoyed until only a few years ago by Oxford and Cambridge Universities may be taken as a typical symbol of the acknowledged state of affairs. In Western Europe, even when university foundations are traceable directly to governmental action, the university remains in effect an association of scholars who have organized themselves for their own purposes rather than an institution set up around a board of trustees, or the equivalent, who seek out scholars suitable for the institution's purposes and employ them. In this latter arrangement, which obtains almost universally in American colleges and universities, governmental and private, although the faculty member may have tenure which guarantees his position for life, his place in the total teaching organization is quite different from that which obtains in Europe.

The European situation is the one in which the Catholic university tradition was formed and of which, more or less, canon law concerning higher education takes cognizance. It is also the situation around which Catholic thought concerning the Church's relationship to higher education has been shaped and to which this thought principally refers. In a way, this thought is relatively simple. The Church is the "Mother of Learning," and of course it is theology which she actively "fosters." Her relationship to the other sciences is hinted at in the relationship of theology to them. Theology is the "queen" of the sciences. In standard usage during the Middle Ages, the Renaissance, and succeeding generations up to the past three or four, "philosophy" commonly meant all that learning beyond grammar and rhetoric which was not medicine, law, or theology and thus included the natural sciences and mathematics and the fields now developed as sociology, economics, engineering (insofar as this was a matter of formal schooling), and the rest. This "philosophy" (which we today would style science-and-philosophy) was the "handmaid" of theology.

It is noteworthy that the dominant imagery in these standard conceptions defines the Church's relationship to learning in womanly terms. The Church's role is relatively passive, even in the case of theology. This science she dominates, but in the sense that she supplies it with its material and first principles from divine revelation and keeps surveillance over what the theologians do with this material, for divine revelation is really hers to preserve and pass on to succeeding generations. She herself does not seem to attack the problems of theology in the truly aggressive fashion which is characteristic of the scientific mind, and of creative theologians themselves, who of course are not the Church. She does not even precisely drive on the theologians in the way in which, for example, the director of basic research in a large and aggressive corporation might drive on his associates. Even when the theologians are fighting for her, her most characteristic reaction seems to be to restrain them when they threaten to go too far or to say something "dangerous" (which may admittedly all the while be perfectly true). The Church here is *das ewige Weib,* the eternal woman around whom battles rage but who herself sits, somehow disengaged, above them.

Naturally, in this setting, theology herself in her relationship to other fields of learning—if not in all her aspects—is thought of as ruling in a womanly way, not as a king or even a prince but as a queen, with the other sciences as satellite handmaids. She is mistress, but Christ Himself is Master. It is He, *"Ipse,* the only one, Christ, King, Head," Who comes "In a flash, at a trumpet crash," Who is "fetched in the storm of his strides." But His Bride, Holy Mother Church, lives the different life that is fitted to her sex, which is thoroughly feminine in a sense somewhere in between the metaphorical and the real.

This womanly economy serves well to define not only the Church's relationship to the original university world but also to frame in a very real way her relationship even today to learning as purveyed in the elementary and secondary schools. For the task of the elementary school and of the secondary school is not to plunge aggressively into the intellectual and scientific life but rather to shape the pupil with the help of the knowledge which is on hand. Precisely what this knowledge itself is remains from certain points of view relatively unimportant—or has up to the present. At the elementary- and secondary-school level, the sciences themselves are not fully assertive and demanding. The development of the pupil's character and integrity enjoys a kind of primacy. At this level knowledge itself or science itself is not being served. The human person is. In this sense the attitude toward the sciences remains personal and feminine, not abstract and masculine. In this personal world the Church is at home.

A personal world is not exclusively feminine, even though, compared to man, woman is more at home in it than she is in an abstract, "objective" world. Hence it is not correct to say that elementary schools and secondary schools necessarily operate in an entirely womanly setting. Obviously, they do not, although, just as obviously, the elementary school is more womanly in its setting, closer to home, than the secondary. The secondary school is in a way transitional. The business of a secondary school for boys, even to some extent in coeducational America, has always been that of toughening the youth for life outside the family in the rougher, more "objective," and more aggressive, life of the tribe.

I wish only to point out that with regard not to its pupils but to the store of knowledge which it is dispensing, the secondary school, and a fortiori the elementary school, can take a rather purely custodial attitude, exploiting knowledge with a view not to the advancement and good of knowledge itself, but with a view to the good of the pupil, to the development of his own integrity. Most good high school teachers, whether in a Catholic school or any other kind of school, feel free from time to time to interject character-building exhortations into their classes, whatever the subject directly under consideration may be. This sort of direct attention to character-building is demanded by the teen-age condition. Without it even abstract subjects cannot be taught to teenagers effectively. The Church finds this attitude toward knowledge congenial to her feminine role, especially since integrity of character will include religious integrity and thus bring her basic concerns more or less directly into play.

The case is somewhat different with higher education. Here, ideally at least, the subjects themselves enforce their own demands. Whereas in secondary school the integrity of the pupil was the prime consideration, here the integrity of the subject becomes paramount. It is ordinarily not very convincing to think of a hard-working youngster in high school as spending himself for a subject: we should more likely describe his situation by saying that he is studying very hard, or is sacrificing himself to his own effort in his studies. But at some point when we move into the field of higher education the subject begins to exert its own claims and we can speak of the young student or scholar as spending *himself* for his *subject*.

At the point where, at least for the very good and devoted students, it becomes possible to say this, higher education in our culture would seem to begin. Perhaps the point can seldom be located exactly. Are the earlier years of undergraduate work too early for it? Is it in graduate school only that students give themselves to a subject, properly speaking? The point will vary, of course, for individuals. But if it cannot always be located precisely, it can be located most of the time within a certain larger period of intellectual

The Apostolate of Secular Arts and Sciences

training—that when a student passes through the college and/or university milieu.

Perhaps some personal commitment or dedication to a subject or field is necessarily the measure of all higher education. If this is so, cultures which do not make it possible for a person to spend himself on a subject, while they may have the equivalent of secondary education in their puberty rites, which take the young boy from the family and equip him with the moral confidence and lore necessary for life in the tribe, cannot be said to have any higher education at all.

Because we are today so acutely aware that knowledge is indefinitely expansible in any given field, we are aware that at some point in a person's education a sense of the incompleteness and continual growth of knowledge must be acquired. The student must become aware at some point that the integrity of a field of knowledge is never a *fait accompli* but rather something like the term of a calculus, something which is worked toward but which will never be fully achieved. An awareness of this condition of knowledge would seem to lie back of the willingness to sacrifice oneself for a subject, and it would seem to be one of the basic acquisitions communicated in higher education, even at the undergraduate level, although active work to further the advance and integration of knowledge is generally reserved for graduate study.

But to support a proper awareness of this incomplete condition of knowledge, a student must have a certain integrity of character and assurance of his own. Otherwise the mere sweep of the new demands on him will be sure to unsettle him. The university or college which communicates these new demands is not, of course, entirely indifferent to the problems of character building in its students, who, it is aware, have matured or are still maturing with varying degrees of rapidity and success. Still, a certain maturity has to be presupposed, if not at the beginning of the college or university career, at least during this career. The student has to be able in some fundamental way to forget himself and his problems, to give himself to the field which he is cultivating as though his own concern with himself were secondary. In this sense, while the secondary school exploits knowledge for the integration of a character (with a view to the still further absorption of knowledge by the person), the institution of higher learning—if not under every aspect, at least in its central concerns—makes claims on the individual in the name of knowledge itself, alleging as its title for these claims the incompleteness of knowledge itself and its need to be served if it is to be maintained in healthy estate.

Such claims cannot be urged in elementary and secondary education because to advertise the incompleteness of knowledge would distract the student in his quest for personal integrity. Thus through the elementary and secondary schools —and to some extent, alas, into the lower reaches of the college or university—we treat knowledge as though it existed in a perfect state which, as a matter of fact, it has by no means achieved and which as a whole it can never achieve. The study of grammar is reduced to normative grammar, with rules more fixed than any scientific grammarian would allow. Geometry is presented as a *fait accompli* rather than as a growing and indefinitely expanding discipline. Physics and chemistry are treated in much the same way. Indeed, a summary, "closed" treatment of knowledge is what the younger pupil not only needs but also wants. He is for the nonce a confirmed rationalist. He wants no complicated answers even to the most complicated questions.

In a certain sense and in certain aspects of development, mankind as a whole has grown definitely in recent days out of the secondary-school and into the higher-education frame of

The Apostolate of Secular Arts and Sciences

mind. One must not be naïve about the naïveté of earlier man, who was a complicated individual and in his own way quite as profound as we in his perceptions and awarenesses. Yet the fact remains that as late as the age of Erasmus knowledge could be thought of as a kind of totality "contained" in its entirety in "the books of the ancients" with a plausibility and lack of reflection which has become impossible today. Palingenesis, the phenomenon whereby the development of each individual of a species is in a certain fashion a parallel of the evolutionary history of the species, seems to apply here. The development in the individual's confrontation of knowledge runs parallel to the development of the race's confrontation. Only as the human race and/or the human individual becomes older is man able to accept with equanimity and even exhilaration explicit awareness of the fact that all natural knowledge is indefinitely expansible. "Human kind/Cannot bear very much reality," T. S. Eliot reminds us, and it can bear less when the individual or the race is young.

To make so much of the development of knowledge as integral to all mature intellectual activity and thus to make research and the development of knowledge paramount in college and university runs somewhat counter to the common understanding of John Henry Newman's view that the university is concerned with teaching, not with research. This view is expressed somewhat guardedly but on the whole firmly in Newman's Preface to *The Idea of a University*, where it is pointed out that "to discover and to teach are two distinct functions" and that "the great discoveries in chemistry and electricity were not made in universities." Newman's concern, however, is not quite the same as our present one. We have been insisting that a feel for knowledge as a growing thing must be communicated in the teaching of any subject at higher educational levels. He is saying that teaching and research are ordinarily carried on separately from each other, a statement with which one might still agree, with some reservations, and which even in Newman's case is in part belied by the plans he had for a chemical laboratory and astronomical observatory at the Catholic University in Dublin. But he is also implying more of a difference between the mentality of a teacher and of an original discoverer than we should be able to admit today, particularly in the upper reaches of the curriculum. The fact is that, despite his magisterial *Essay on the Development of Christian Doctrine*, Newman was not so acutely and circumstantially aware as we are of the developmental character of all human knowledge. During his lifetime the human mind was just entering into the historical phase of its development where it would become intensely and reflexively aware of the fact of development itself. While his thought is maturing and moving toward the awareness which we have today, there lingers a tendency to divorce teaching and research which is in great part a relict of the ages preceding his own. If Newman were alive today, a mere glance at textbooks in any subject ranged in chronological order over the past few generations, and fitted with notes on the careers of their authors, would make inescapable the connection between advance in research and university teaching.

II

The problem of the Church's relation to higher education is thus rather different from the problem of her relation to other education. What happens when the Church, the Bride and Mother interested not so much in science as in her children, enters as active sponsor into the intellectual world—perhaps the most aggressive of all worlds—not by "mothering" universities as she did in the Middle Ages, but rather by undertaking to set them up as she has within the present

The Apostolate of Secular Arts and Sciences

United States, in an age when the frontiers of knowledge are spectacularly expanding on all sides?

Canon law does not give many cues here. It states (Canon 1379, § 2) that if the public universities of a nation or region are not "imbued with Catholic doctrine and sensibility" it is desirable that a Catholic university be founded. An earlier canon (1113) recognizing parents' responsibility for education of their children does not attend to the cultivation of knowledge itself but only to the education which parents are obliged to provide for their children in matters "religious and moral, as well as physical and civic." This statement is in keeping with the motherly and personal concerns of the Church. It prescribes an attitude toward persons rather than toward learning. By the same token, however, it does not give much help with regard to the question here being considered concerning Catholic universities in the United States. These canons leave off where our question begins: When the Church as such undertakes not merely a chaplaincy in a university but the management of a university, what sort of commitment does she have to the secular learning which the university must necessarily profess?

The problem has not been thought through because the Church's present educational program in the United States was in the first instance a necessity dictated by a practical situation. In most of the United States, colleges and universities—as well as elementary and secondary schools—were at one time in effect Protestant. This was true even of state-supported institutions until fairly recently. The still sacrosanct term used to characterize tax-supported educational institutions in the United States is "nonsectarian," and this term was originally applied to indicate that such institutions did not discriminate among the various "sects" of Protestants, but were Protestant in a generic, nondiscriminatory way. Catholics, Jews, and others were usually left quite out of consideration. Faced with this situation, Catholics naturally wished their own educational institutions, where, to use Matthew Arnold's words describing similar situations in Europe, "religion and the matters mixed up with religion" were taught by Catholics. Under these conditions, with or without the recommendations of canon law, Catholic colleges and universities were inevitable to protect the individual's rights.

But the size and success of the ensuing educational program, as well as the development of learning itself, have produced a situation which is new for the Church. When Catholic education has reached the degree of development which it is reaching in the United States, it poses questions as to whether the Church's commitment to secular learning in the institutions which she has founded is determined purely by a tutelary position she must take regarding her members. Does she become involved in secular subjects merely as the result of an unusual crisis? Or is she really more involved in them by her very nature than Catholics themselves have hitherto been aware? Does she have some reason not merely to purvey the secular subjects as they are known now but to advance knowledge of them on every front? Will the advance of secular knowledge be of service to her in the achievement of her mission, or is it even perhaps in some way part of her mission? It is imperative that thinking concerning the nature of the Church's commitment to secular knowledge be done today in the United States and elsewhere, and it seems well that it be done in public, for there is really no other way to do it. It is of the nature of the academic world itself to disseminate an understanding of problems and to encourage thought about them.

When thinking about the present problem is minimal, there are certain considerations which are vaguely assumed to take care of the question as to what the Church's commitment to secular education is, if not directly the answer to the question. One such consideration, the defensive, simply stops with the knowledge that the Church has established universities and colleges to keep Catholics from frequenting non-Catholic schools. This is taken as a fact which involves no particular problems. Or it may be conjoined with a second consideration, the prestige consideration, which rejoices in the establishment of universities and colleges because they prove to the incredulous that the Church is not antiscientific. Related to this is a third consideration, that of infiltration: the Church is supposed to favor the cultivation of secular knowledge by her members simply in order that when a Catholic becomes the peer of others in a specialized field, his religious opinions may get a hearing on the basis of his demonstrable intellectual competence. A fourth consideration thinks of secular subjects as lures: with the aid of courses in literature and mathematics and even electronics—or fly fishing or automobile driving, for anything at all will do here—the Church gets Catholics and/or non-Catholics within earshot only to provide them with Christian dogma, or at least to expose them to it, and this is all. A fifth consideration can be called sacramental: through her universities and colleges the Church somehow Christianizes the secular subjects themselves, even, for example, meteorology or nuclear physics. What might be called the redemptive consideration is a sixth: since non-Catholic interpretations of the field of knowledge as a whole fail to do justice to the full Catholic view and to truth, the Church must somehow lay hold of the entire field of knowledge in order to straighten out matters.

None of these vaguely assumed considerations quite take care of the question in hand. The defensive consideration is purely negative and anti-intellectual: it implies that, provided there were no non-Catholic universities, the Church would be just as well off and just as satisfied if secular knowledge were not cultivated at all. Such an implication might seem to draw support from canon law as just cited above (Canon 1379, § 2), but it does not, for the canon does not say that it is desirable to found Catholic universities only if and when competition arises, but rather that it is advisable if existing universities are not Catholic in outlook. Historically, the first universities were Catholic in outlook, so that the canon supposes that other universities have risen in competition with or in addition to those of Catholic outlook rather than vice versa.

The second or prestige consideration is equally negative and perhaps even more anti-intellectual: if one's only purpose in being scientific is to prove that one is not antiscientific, one *is* antiscientific. The true scientific drive has quite different sources from this vainglorious one. The third consideration seems as opprobrious as all infiltration tactics. It depends on concealment, so much so that those who rely on it in their thinking seldom state it outright. It seems impossible to imagine a distinguished Catholic economist, layman or priest, studying economics only to gain a hearing for his theology, and preposterous to imagine his avowing such a warped motive to his colleagues. The fourth consideration —the lure—presents the same difficulty, being equally meretricious: in a sense, of course, the natural world is ordered to the supernatural, and all creation is for God, but this does not mean that in itself His natural creation, including the sciences which it generates, merits no respect, that secular subjects can be taken up or jettisoned like so much bait for fishing. The fifth consideration is interesting, although it presents a great many problems: How does one go about Christianizing meteorology or nuclear physics? The sixth consideration presents difficulties, too, for how does the Church straighten out aberrations in natural knowledge? Yet the fifth and sixth considerations do, it seems, hold the promise of providing some answer to our question, What is the Church's commitment to secular learning?

This question can be broken down into two related questions: Can the Church commit herself to secular learning and, if so, how? If not, can she administer a university without such commitment? Any answer to these questions must be founded on the admission that the Church's concern with secular disciplines themselves can never be quite direct. Even her concern with theology, as has been hinted above, is less direct than her concern with the Scriptures and tradition, which are of God and out of which theology grows. Her role in the cosmos is defined by her relationship to God: she is the Bride of Christ and our Holy Mother. As a real Bride and Mother, she is related primarily to persons and only secondarily to things. This means that her relationship to the sciences, which in themselves are determined not by persons but by things or "objects" (or, to speak another way, are "about subjects"), is mediated by her relationship to individual human beings.

The theorem thus seems to obtain that when the Church commits herself actively to secular subjects, she does so only through the personal commitment of her children devoted to secular subjects. But this theorem does not solve our questions. Rather, it reorganizes them into two further questions: First, what end is served when the Church commits a priest or religious to a secular subject as his scholarly or scientific vocation? Secondly, does a Catholic lay scholar have as a Catholic any commitment to his subject which he would not have if he were not a Catholic? We can take up these questions in succession.

III

A layman or laywoman gives his or her life to the Church normally through his family or his own circle of acquaintances. The priest or religious, on the other hand, gives his or her life directly to God and His Church so that in a certain sense for him the members of the Church herself become his family. The layman belongs to the Church directly, of course, but he is not at the disposition of the Church. He is at the disposition of his family or the equivalent of his family, those in the world to whom he is in one way or another tied or obligated. The priest or religious, on the other hand, not only belongs to the Church but is at the direct disposition of the Church. The disposition may, in some cases, be restricted: a monk with a vow of stability is, under normal circumstances, supposed to live his life in his monastery and not to be sent elsewhere for permanent residence. But this is a restriction in the range which the Church's disposition may have; it is not a restriction by commitment to something or someone other than the Church herself.

Because of the relationship of the priest or religious to the Church, the first question, What end is served when the Church commits a priest or religious to a secular subject as his scholarly vocation? is a particularly acute one. For the priest or religious is committed to the Church, and his commitment to the secular subject now exists inside his religious vocation, not as something superadded, but as a form of that vocation. Moreover, by committing to a secular subject one who is already completely committed to her, the Church herself commits herself to the subject more directly than otherwise. The commitment of the Church is still effected through an individual person, but the commitment is direct in that the Church through hierarchical or religious superiors directly brings about the commitment of the person in question. It is precisely the existence of this kind of commitment on a large scale which is new and distinctive of the Church's development in the present-day United States. Moreover, as Catholic universities and colleges come of age and begin to pull their own scholarly and scientific weight, it is a commitment which is growing daily.

In the case of some secular subjects, such as, for example, philosophy or literature or history, one might argue that the subjects are so closely allied with theology and so inevitably involved with the matter of revelation that to touch them is, in effect, to touch religious matters. In such cases, one might argue, priests and religious are devoted to these subjects because it would seem better to have in charge of the field persons with theological training or at least with special dedication to the Church as the depository of revelation. This implies that such subjects should always be taught by priests or religious, and therefore that laymen are teaching them only by default. This view is sometimes taken, explicitly or implicitly, by those unfamiliar with the actual history of Catholic education, and Newman's *The Idea of a University* is in great part an attempt to put the record straight for the party in Ireland who wished a university run on these principles, patterned after a seminary with only priests for instructors.

But the view will not stand inspection. First of all, the Church has no mandate at all to put anyone "in charge" of a field of secular learning. Even should she want to, she cannot even certify to a person's competence in such fields, except insofar as they may stray into the field of revelation. Secondly, higher education has never existed on these terms in any Catholic culture. For priests to monopolize subjects other than theology has been unknown on any representative scale in any Catholic university tradition. Despite a prevalent impression to the contrary, even in the Middle Ages professors of philosophy were quite commonly neither priests nor students for the priesthood. Furthermore, a pattern of education restricting to priests the teaching of subjects tangent to theology is utterly preposterous in the learned world today and not even remotely feasible. Not only would there be always an insufficiency of priests qualified to staff departments of such subjects, but to mobilize priests so as to silence competent laymen in these fields, which have always been developed chiefly by laymen, would certainly work to the detriment of knowledge itself.

Further still, the real patterning in American Catholic education does not follow these lines. In American Catholic colleges and universities priests and religious are deployed pretty thoroughly through all the fields of learning, from philosophy to chemistry and from eighteenth century French literature to geophysics. And, although individual priests or religious in any field at all may be persons of some distinction, the original contributions of priests and religious to learning in the United States, it seems very likely, are greater in the physical sciences, which are presumably more remote from theology, than in philosophy and literature or in most of the other humanities, which presumably have more direct theological implications. This would indicate that it is impossible to demonstrate that the Church commits a priest or religious to a secular subject because of the subject's possible tangential reference to theology or revelation rather than because of the subject's intrinsic worth in itself.

It will not do at this point to deceive ourselves by thinking that the commitment of priests or religious to secular subjects in the United States has come about in a fashion any less pragmatic than is actually the case. The Church felt a need to establish a Catholic milieu for higher education, and the only practical way to implement a program of Catholic higher education proved to be the mobilization of religious and of priests to organize and at first in great part to staff such institutions. Higher education necessarily involved secular subjects, and thus it was that priests and religious became involved in these things.

From this point of view our question can be answered by saying that the end sought by the commitment of priests and religious to secular subjects in higher education has been the Christianization of the intellectual milieu. But when we move past this generalization, the question seems hardly answered. For how is this Christianization accomplished? By having priests and religious as administrators? By salting the various departments with at least a sprinkling of priests and religious who make the Church present in a special way? By personal extracurricular contacts? (If this is the aim, why have priests for anything other than chaplains?—then they could devote their full time to personal extracurricular contacts.)

The very fact that such questions have not been thought through is indicative. For this shows that the Church is at home in this educational situation and can, as a matter of fact and quite independently of theory, work with it.

IV

The Christian is at home in the world of secular learning. Indeed, it is important to note how peculiarly Christian the effective rapprochement between religious and secular subjects really is. Other "world religions" are not like this. With the possible exception of certain types of law, Islam has never been friendly to any secular learning not strictly in the direct service of theology. The outburst of intellectual creativity among the Arabs in the ninth to twelfth centuries which produced Alfarabius, Avicenna, and Averroës had its flowering not in Islam but in Christian scholastic philosophy. In Islam it was smothered by the Koran and Islamic law. Until the end of the last century "The study of philosophy had been prohibited in Egypt as antagonistic to religion, and logic had been condemned as a means to atheism," Ahmed Fouad El Ehwany explains in a recent issue of *Philosophy*

East and West. Recently in Egypt, Mustafa Abd El Razik has made a great name for himself as a daring thinker by teaching formal logic and reading texts from Avicenna's works of ten centuries ago. Islamic foreign students at Catholic universities in the United States are uniformly nonplused at the sight of priests and religious, who seem dedicated to religion in a way like that of a mullah, actually undergoing secular education, and are utterly bewildered at the idea of their engaging in educational work. Hinduism and Buddhism have not generated the close association with secular science that has been common in Christianity especially since the medieval universities. Neither has Confucianism nor Shinto, although Confucianism has perhaps the better record here.

Basically, the reason for the difference in the case of Christianity is the fact of the Incarnation, which has rooted the Church in the natural world, for the Second Person of the Blessed Trinity took to Himself a human nature, not a supernature. The matter in His body, we now know, was actually billions of years old, prepared in God's Providence over this incredibly long period of time for its final stages in the human organism and in the body of Jesus Christ. Even more profoundly, and certainly more spectacularly, than earlier Christians could have imagined, the Incarnation "involves" God Himself in the natural world. The fullness of time has proved to be even fuller than one might have imagined, as the natural world has proved to be not only billions of times more voluminous but also vastly more developmental in its very structure than any strict Aristotelian could have allowed.

If through the Incarnation the Church is committed to cosmic history, by the very same token she is committed to secular learning, for secular learning is not a thing apart from cosmic history, something superadded to it, but rather something within that history which develops in articulation with earlier events in the same history, to protract and fulfill them. When the cosmos has attained a certain degree of maturity, God creates the first human soul and infuses it into the matter prepared for it. As the human race develops, human understanding and learning develop, for learning, whether that of letters or of science, does not exist full-blown at the beginning of human civilization. It is essentially not only something which puts in its seminal appearance with man himself at a certain time in cosmic history—some five to ten billion years from the beginning of the universe we know—but also something which has a measured growth. The growth of knowledge protracts the growth of the cosmos itself which has given birth to man, for through this growth of knowledge the cosmos comes to its own fuller and fuller maturity, in which it becomes aware of itself and its relationship to God.

Learning develops with man, and has in the past few generations reached the stage where we are learning to write the history of learning itself. We have found that man in any given culture at any period of time knows in terms of a complex of concepts which belong to that culture and time. The concepts may represent truth well enough, and very accurately, but they also do so selectively. And the particular kind of selection in its cognitive approach to reality which a culture typically makes dates the culture unmistakably. There could be no mistaking a medieval European tractate on cosmology or even on the soul for a Japanese one of the same period or for an ancient Egyptian one or for a modern neoscholastic one. Each treatise would give evidence of knowledge unexploited, and often unexploitable, by the other.

This cultural differentiation in approaches to knowledge can be recognized on a quite small time-scale within a single civilization. In some universities it is the practice to give students of English language and literature a "dating" test in which a brief passage of prose—and almost any kind will do—is to be assigned to the period of time to which it belongs, and that within a few decades. The clues are more than stylistic, of course; the concepts in play in the passage are themselves clues, as are also the concepts which are not in play, for one can date thinking by the knowledge which it does not exhibit as well as by the knowledge which it does. Men today know in terms of complexes of concepts most of which the men of a few thousand years ago had not yet learned to form, although the experience of men gathered thousands of years ago has gone into their formation.

In this way thinking itself is dated, situated within the frame of cosmic history. Thus, to take an example from the foregoing paragraph, the sentence "This cultural differentiation in approaches to knowledge can be recognized on a quite small time-scale within a single civilization," we find here any number of clues situating this type of thinking well within the twentieth century. "Cultural differentiation" is a term registering a way of thinking generated quite recently by anthropology. The concept of an "approach to knowledge" is definitely post-Newtonian in its spatialization of knowledge, which it represents as existing in a kind of "field," and it is twentieth century in its preoccupation with process. "Timescale" is a product of a civilization which takes utterly for granted quantified measurements in terms of charts and graphs, hence quite recent. And the kind of interest discernible in the whole of the sentence bespeaks a preoccupation with evolution not found until quite recent years. The sentence belongs to a certain era in the natural history of human thought.

The Church's own history is involved with the natural history of human thought. The Church's history is sacred, but it is a sacred history lived out within the history of the natural cosmos—even more so than the history of ancient Israel, which was partially insulated from secular history by the theocratic organization of its entire society and by its minuscule size. Because she is part of cosmic history, the Church coexists with the secular and could not exist without it. She is involved in an incalculable number of ways with the nations, with the affairs of men, personal, domestic, political, cultural in any number of senses, and of course intellectual. Indeed, she is particularly involved with the history of the human intellect, including its secular history, for two reasons. First, this history is the history of the cosmos par excellence, since man is the cosmos granted consciousness of itself in the sense that he is the point in the cosmos where God has inserted spirituality, where the material world enters on its natural fulfillment by, in a way, possessing itself through a spiritual being which both transcends it and is part of it, and for which it has prepared itself. (It might be mentioned here that the history of voluntary decisions, arrived at within the framework made possible by intellectual development, is not so much the history of the cosmos as it is the history of individual persons, for one's decisions are independent of other persons in a way in which one's understanding can never be. The history of an individual's free decisions is thus his own history par excellence, for it tells what has really happened to him, not exteriorly but in his deepest interior: not an individual's knowledge, but his decisions tell what *he* is.)

Secondly, the Church is particularly involved with the history of the human intellect because the Church is the extension in time and space of the Word of God, of God's own personal expression and manifestation of His understanding of Himself. It was the Word of God Who became man; it was Intelligence Who took to Himself flesh. Her special relationship to the Word of God leaves a mark on the Church. Her mysterious alliance with knowledge of every sort is something which is quite evident, even when the details of its working out remain in great part a puzzle.

The special relationship of the Church to natural knowledge, and thus some of the issues at stake in the commitment of her members, lay and clerical, to natural knowledge, can be seen rather clearly in terms of the American university structure. It has been pointed out above that American universities differ from the traditional European ones in that the European are typically associations of teachers or scholars or scientists (or sometimes of students) organized for the implementation of their own professional work. The original universities of Paris and Oxford and Cambridge were organized in a way comparable to a local unit of the American Association of University Professors rather than to an American university proper, which can in a sense exist by virtue of its extra-academic board of trustees without any teachers at all, and, so far as that goes, without even any literacy at all, for it is not likely that any laws require that members of boards of trustees be able to read and write. The board of trustees—or its equivalent, whatever the name—is an extra-academic group to whom the university is "chartered" and who see to the hiring of the professionals who make a university work.

As has been seen, it has been the existence of this pattern in the United States which has made the Catholic church-affiliated college and university possible to an extent never known in the most "officially" Catholic countries which the world has ever seen. The Church comes on the scene in American college and university life by setting up boards of trustees. The Church herself is, of course, never really the board of trustees, nor does she "control" the board of trustees and everything within the college or university in the sense suggested in the ordinary paranoid myth of a monolithic, totalitarian Catholicism. It is impossible, for example, even in the case of the Catholic University of America, which is supported directly by the American episcopacy as a whole, for the American bishops or the Church through them to "control" teaching at the university in such a way as to subject it entirely to the magisterium of the Church. What goes on at the university as a whole is one thing, and what goes on in the magisterium is another. By setting up a university the episcopacy has implemented the pursuit of learning, about which pursuit the episcopacy as such has nothing directly to say save where faith or morals are somehow in question. The division of roles here is rather sharper than the division between the faculty of a secular university and the secular board of trustees.

Inasmuch as the Church through a board of trustees which she sets up is responsible, indirectly, for the operation of a university, is such a board any more committed to the advance of secular learning than a board of trustees made up of secular personnel under purely secular auspices—a board, let us say, of bankers, manufacturers, and stockbrokers gathered under no particular religious auspices? The answer, we intuitively feel, would have to be Yes. Why? Because somehow or other the Church is more directly involved in this advancement than are individual bankers or manufacturers or stockbrokers. They may, incidentally, for personal or business reasons be interested in one or another field of knowledge. Occasionally, one or another might be intensely interested in the advancement of all knowledge. But the Church is *involved* in the advancement of all knowledge, for this is something which affects the *spiritual* activity of the human race.

There is something in learning as such which relates it to the Church more than to banking, manufacturing, or finance. As the Church is Catholic, exercising a presence through the whole of reality, so learning has a special kind of infinity of its own: any of it may touch anything. Atom physics is big with consequences for man's understanding of himself and his place in the universe. So is linguistics or biochemistry or English literature. All of these furnish matter for profound reflection. And, as the depository of the revelation given by the Word of God, it is the Church's business to reflect— much more than it is that of the banker as such or the manufacturer as such or the stockbroker as such. The Church must reflect on the meaning of the Word in the universe, the real physical universe with whose being and manifestations the various sciences are concerned. Unthinking persons sometimes talk of the Church's teaching as though it were exclusively a matter of purveying neatly packaged formulae which are stored before and after utterance in a kind of Univac. It is true that there are formulae which directly express the great truths of faith, but these do not work independently of reflection. There is no way to package thought. Formulae are generators of thought. Even the catechism is a starting point for reflection. Thus the recent revision of the Baltimore Catechism changed the answer which had long been given to so basic a question as "Why did God make me?" The earlier answer, it was found, led to irrelevant or misleading reflections.

By her reflection on divine revelation in terms which come into being within history (the history of the human mind, the history of man thinking) the Church effects the Christianization of the intellectual milieu. In Chapter 4 the interaction of secular knowledge and revealed religion has been discussed in some of its general aspects. But this interaction is not merely general. It takes place on a myriad of fronts simultaneously as the web of concepts by which each human culture manages contact with reality adapts itself to new situations and needs, and as the various webs representative of the various human cultures over the face of the earth become

The Apostolate of Secular Arts and Sciences

themselves more and more woven together in our own day. To understand in detail the ways in which the Church uses new conceptual developments to exploit her store of revelation and make it more accessible and understandable to man would take whole volumes and would demand an exhaustive knowledge of such fields as sociology, semantics, linguistics, and depth psychology, as well as of the history of ideas itself and of theology. Nevertheless some beginnings for such understanding have been made in the work of Albert Gelin, Jean Daniélou, Henri de Lubac, Yves Congar, and others.

The Church's need to reflect on divine revelation in terms which come and are coming into being daily within intellectual history seems to be the ultimate ground of her entrance into formal education at its highest levels. It is also the basic justification for the commitment of priests and religious to secular fields of learning (although, as we have seen, it may not be the primary operative reason which effects this commitment in most individual cases). The Church needs to be present to secular learning and to have it present to her in order to realize her mission as the Mystical Body of Christ, extending the effects of the Incarnation to all her members and, so far as she can, to all men—which certainly means to all the reaches of their intellectual activity. In fulfilling her mission to bring the entire world to Christ, the Church must reflect not only on divine revelation but also upon creation itself. Today, when knowledge of creation is expanding at ever increasing speed, more than ever she needs to be present at the frontiers of knowledge, to make this knowledge her own at its sources—for the very good reason that it is precisely knowledge at its sources, new knowledge, which is most affecting the most alert human minds.

Perhaps an instance illustrating the need here can be found in the questions which are now put commonly to Catholic theologians concerning the relationship of the Incarnation and the Redemption to the rest of the universe, if parts of this universe are inhabited. The only answers producible so far have an ineffectual and unreal ring. They seem "canned," not vitally related to the actual problem. They are generally based on an old Newtonian cosmology in which matter has no history but is considered quite independently of any time factor. In such a cosmology life is a phenomenon unrelated to time. Other intelligent creatures would pose no problems of an order different from those now posed for us. The entire time factor which permeates modern cosmology is left out of consideration. Yet life is a part of creation which appears only after a long preparation in time. Man appears after a still longer time and a correspondingly longer elaboration of the structure of matter. Would life on other planets have emerged at another time in the history of the material universe and by that very factor be a different sort of thing? I am sure I do not know, and I doubt that anyone does. Yet this is the *type* of problem which has to be thought about if a Christian approach to modern cosmology is to be real and meaningful. The time factor so essential to Einsteinian physics, not to mention the Heisenberg indeterminacy principle, has caught up with theology and opened a new phase in Catholic thought.

The Church has a stake in the totality of human knowledge, for it is in terms of this totality that she must explain her message to the world, and, indeed, that her members must hold her message in their own consciousness. Because of the relationship of revelation to natural knowledge, and to growing natural knowledge, it seems quite accurate to state that one reason why the Church is devoted to higher education in the secular subjects is to educate herself in what is absolutely essential for her mission. In particular, if the clergy were totally unaware of intellectual developments in secular subjects, it would seem quite impossible, humanly speaking, for them to present the truths of faith without distortion and even heresy. We must never forget that in their mistaken assumptions in the realm of physics, seventeenth century Catholic theologians had become confused enough to believe that the Scriptures taught that the sun went around the earth. Here a theological error was occasioned by a faulty understanding of natural science. Similar errors at the time of the discovery of evolution were for the most part fortunately averted, but not in the case of every theologian. Some theological manuals can still, by playing "safe" in matters of evolution, give serious scandal to the informed and trained mind.

Because of the Church's special stake in the totality of human knowledge, because it is important to her that the cosmos in which Christ became incarnate be understood as well and as thoroughly and as soon as possible, the person who as a priest or religious is dedicated in a special way to the Church and who is committed to scholarship and teaching is thus committed to his field not only as much as the non-Catholic scholar or scientist but just a little more because of the additional commitment which the Church herself has and which he in a special way shares. He is dedicated to mastering the subject or area of knowledge to which he is devoted and by the same token to advancing and propagating it. He may, of course, for all sorts of reasons drop the subject for another or for other types of activity, just as any other person might do. But while he is dedicated to it, he is dedicated to it utterly.

In this setting, how about his priestly vocation? Where is his apostolate? Is it entirely indirect and incidental—a matter of fortuitous contacts where the subject of religion can be brought in and direct pastoral help provided to individual souls? Such an apostolate is, of course, a real and normal thing for most priests and religious devoted to higher education.

But it cannot be their chief apostolate for reasons already given above, and because, if it were, the more a person was occupied with his subject, the less apostolic he would be, so that the apostolic ideal would be for him to drop his field of learning entirely and devote himself to the pastoral ministry. Moreover, it would be wrong for the Church to spend her priests and religious this way, devoting them to work which takes them away from the directly religious. And yet she has done this for centuries, and she does it still, not only in the United States now on a massive scale, but on a lesser scale in Europe and India and China and Africa when occasion offers. The apostolate of fortuitous contacts must remain an incidental, if a real and sometimes fruitful one.

The essential apostolate of the priest or religious who is scholar or scientist is more profound and calls for a great degree of dedication and self-abnegation. For this apostolate is realized when the priest or religious integrates within his own person the knowledge which he is pursuing and developing in his field. It is good for the cause of Christ, for His Church, that natural knowledge on a scale both massive and particularized coexist with the special participation in Christ which priests and religious are given. This coexistence can be achieved only within individual persons, in whom secular knowledge, with its grasp on the created universe, and Catholic faith, hope and charity, with their grasp on God, are simultaneously present.

Such integration is sure to be edifying, to have its apostolic effect, but this effect is achieved in a personal way, not by transfer of prestige from one field of knowledge to another. The apostolic effect of the activity of the late Father James B. Macelwane, S.J., in the field of geophysics was not achieved through a wide circulation of his theological or religious views made possible by his eminence as a seismologist and his role in establishing the science of geophysics in the

United States in educational institutions both non-Catholic and Catholic. Few of Father Macelwane's associates, Catholic or non-Catholic, had occasion for long religious talks with the man. His apostolate was one of presence: as a person, he manifested the association of a vast scientific knowledge with a total and unshakable Catholic faith, joined with hope and charity and shown within the framework of a life specially given to Christ in His Church. Fellow scientists might have resented it if he had used seismology, ever so cautiously and astutely, to implement religious or theological designs. True scientists do not like their science to be "used." They respect it and reverence it for just what it is and are jealous of its own integrity. But they cannot take umbrage at what a man *is:* if he is a scientist and a Catholic priest, the effect cannot but be impressive. Such a person is fulfilling the highest vocation of a Christian. He is a witness (the Greek word is *martyros,* martyr) to Christ. His presence becomes Christ's presence. A witness is ready to talk when asked, but what matters is not the words he utters, but the person that he is. For it is not words, or even beliefs, but persons themselves who call for credence.

V

What has been said about the vocation of the priest or religious dedicated to the teaching and to the scholarly or scientific pursuit of secular subjects applies equally, *mutatis mutandis,* to the Catholic layman or laywoman devoted to the same life. The apostolate in both cases is one of presence. I have discussed the problem first in terms of priests or religious because this in a way intensifies the issue of the sacred vis-à-vis the secular since their lives are so evidently and even spectacularly tied up with the life of the Church herself. But the lives of the laity are just as really and profoundly tied up with the life of the Church, only in a different way, and the issue of the sacred vis-à-vis the secular is just as real to them, if again in a different way.

The presence exercised by the layman or laywoman is both like and different from that of a priest or religious. Like priests and religious, laymen and laywomen are witnesses to Christ, whether they are teaching or working in a Catholic or non-Catholic milieu. More often than the priest, the layman will be working in a non-Catholic setting, where, it goes without saying, his Catholic faith should under normal circumstances be a fact manifest and obvious, if quite extracurricular. But the type of witness born by the layman has its own special character. It testifies to the solidarity of the Church with mankind itself and with the natural world in a way that the witness or priests and religious does not do. One can see the point by imagining an impossible Church made up of only priests and religious. Something would certainly be essentially lacking in the way in which Christ Himself was made present to the world. Laymen have roots in the secular which enable Christ to utilize them to establish His kingdom within natural creation in a way impossible without a devoted laity. This means that a person outside the Church who feels a layman's presence often notices and is affected by what the layman does more than by what a priest might do. He cannot make the priest's activities his own with the ease with which he can make the layman's his own. The priest seems remote, precisely because of his special dedication to God.

Some remoteness here is necessary and good. For God is holy, and the notion of holiness is associated with remoteness of a sort. The Hebrew word for holy, *kadosh,* which the angels sing before the throne of God, at root means "separated." Being set apart is therefore a kind of condition reminding one of God's set-apartness. The layman, too, is set apart, for he is a member of the Church, the *Ecclesia,* the

The Apostolate of Secular Arts and Sciences

body of persons "called out" from the world. Yet the layman is not so entirely called out from the secular as the priest is. He has personal commitments to the secular which the priest has transmuted into personal commitment of himself to the entire church. These commitments are an asset, for by keeping the layman with one foot in the secular, they give this secular world from which layman and priest or religious are called, a special relationship to the sacred.

The layman's role here is particularly connected with what has been said earlier (in Chapter 3) about the meaning of the term Catholic, "through-the-whole." The Church's life is to penetrate the whole of human history and activity like leaven. She is to grow into that which surrounds her. Her activity on human society is a growth from the interior—from the interior of individuals and from the interior of human society itself. The layman's presence in areas inside human society not ordinarily accessible to priests is one of the things which implements this interior growth and thus the Catholicity of the Church. And the layman is so present—in the social life of other laymen, their family interests, and their intellectual life and achievements as tangent to these things—not by default of priests or religious but because it is his business precisely as a layman to live these "contacts." Through him, then, the Church reaches into the whole and realizes her Catholicity, and that in a diversity of ways which God alone can enumerate.

VI

Apropos of the activity of both Catholic laity and clergy in higher education, certain concluding reflections touching on the relationship of the secular and the sacred seem necessary.

The relationship of secular learning to Catholic apologetic is always a delicate thing, like the relationship itself between reason and faith. It goes without saying that no secular science must ever be distorted or subjected to the least violence for apologetic purposes. Scientists with religious convictions have not always observed this rule in the past, although their violations of it have perhaps most often been unintentional. The difficulties here can, of course, be very real, for it is not always clear what is implied by the truths of faith, and it is harmful to the cause of the Catholic faith to make it imply more than it really does, just as it is harmful to make it imply less. To make the faith imply more than it does is not a virtue but a sin, although in the case of many good people the sin is hardly imputable for want of awareness.

A good example of the workings of misplaced piety which wants divine revelation to say more than it does can be seen in connection with the developments in the science of geology during the past two centuries turning on the work of Lamarck, Lyell, and others. From ancient classical times men had attempted to account for the existence of mountains and seas in terms of catastrophes in nature. According to the standard ancient view set down in Aristotelian cosmology, the terrestrial globe should have been made up of concentric perfect spheres of earth, water, air, and fire, in that order. The fact that it was not, that in places the earth jutted out above the water, that water was stored in springs under the earth, and that both water and earth, forming as they did the undersurface of the sphere of air, wreaked havoc with the "natural" regularity of this sphere, was accounted for by "violence." Something out of the ordinary course of events had caused this untoward condition in the central sphere in the cosmos, the earth on which we live.

Long after the earth-centered cosmology of Aristotle and Ptolemy had been replaced by the Copernican cosmology in the minds of educated men, the catastrophic theory of the formation of mountains and seas lingered on, in great part less by reason of any stubborn attachment to the Greek spherical cosmology than by a simple default of any other theory to account in detail for geophysical phenomena. After modern geology began with the work of the Catholic bishop Niels Steensen, catastrophism began to be replaced by uniformitarianism, so called because it accounted, as we do today, for the present condition of the cosmos in terms of operations of nature not essentially different from those which are at present observable.

But meanwhile, in the minds of many Christians, Catholics and Protestants alike, catastrophism had taken on a religious meaning. It seemed a short cut to a knowledge of the existence and power of God if one could have in the universe catastrophic occurrences which had no explanation other than His direct intervention. Hence we find certain ill-advised religious cosmologists caught in a long series of successive retreats, defending on more or less apologetic grounds the divine intervention at points which one after the other became untenable. God had put into the earth the fossils on which geologists such as Lyell relied simply to confound such stupid geologists. Or the fossils on mountaintops washed there during the Deluge. And so on. Attempts to "harmonize" geology with Genesis such as no serious Catholic scriptural scholar today would tolerate for a moment multiplied as never before.

Such attempts are relatively rare today even on non-scholarly levels. Ways of accounting for the form of the history of the world given in Genesis have been found which are much more tenable and real. Yet catastrophism persists in a mitigated form. As Herbert Spencer remarked, it was lingering in biology long after it had disappeared from geology. And it lingers still. Unfortunately, certain textbooks by Catholics still maintain it for the origins of life, which we are told (for religious, not philosophical reasons) could not arise on the earth by natural processes without some "special" intervention of God. Or we are given to understand that God's creation of the first human soul and His infusion of it into matter which had been prepared over a period of some five to ten billion years to receive it is more "special" an intervention, less "natural," than His creation of your soul or mine occasioned by the juncture of two germ cells.

Resort to catastrophism in cosmology for religious reasons is a classic example of the distortion of a science for apologetic purposes, and a good example of the havoc wreaked by such distortions. It undoubtedly weakened the faith of many who, precocious in their insights into physical phenomena, knew that what was here being said to "defend" the Christian religion could not be true and hence concluded that the religion itself was suspect—concluded mistakenly, for the Catholic faith does not depend on the reasons assigned by individual defenders, who frequently enough go far beyond the Church in their explicitness concerning her teachings.

We can learn humbly from the errors of others—although one might conjecture that, since few of us are as humble as we might be, perhaps after all we shall not learn. God's cause is served by truth, humbly arrived at and humbly accepted, not by conclusions generated out of our own desire for security. If we are to say that God's "special" intervention is required for the origin of life from nonliving matter—a statement which was not credited by St. Augustine or St. Thomas Aquinas and which is far closer to Pasteur and to Thomas Henry Huxley than to the Scriptures and the actual teaching of the Church—where will we be if the present experiments with the synthesizing of amino acids or with deoxyribonucleic acid result in the production of life in the laboratory, as it appears more and more likely they may? Discrediting of a no longer tenable position when this has been associated with God's revelation inevitably both discredits this revelation itself in the eyes of unbelievers and spreads confusion among even believers.

One cannot escape the impression that resort to catastrophism, and similar distortions of secular science, are due to some unhealthy fear that, without our help, without our own particular explanation bolstered in its own peculiar ways, divine revelation is untenable. It should be noted that the psychological difficulties which resulted in catastrophism are not derivative directly from any proclamation or condemnation by the Church herself but are due to fearsome concerns entertained, perhaps often subconsciously, by the devout—and shared by the scoffer, who feels that *if* he believed he, too, would have to resort to such a distorted apologetic to protect his own security.

In the last analysis, perhaps the greatest enemy of the loyal Catholic committed wholeheartedly to secular learning is unhealthy fear. He should, of course, have the fear of the Lord which is the beginning of wisdom, and a healthy respect and reverence for the authority of the Church. But when the claims of truth in his science are concerned, he should not fear for his own reputation among even his fellow Catholics who may be ill informed. He should not confuse the authority of the Church with his own subconscious promptings and a desire for universal approval among men. Nor should he make of decisions of the Church more than the Church herself does.

Above all, the Catholic concerned with secular learning must beware of transferring to other than theological fields concepts and attitudes which are proper to theology. Catholic theology is subject ultimately to the authority of the Church, for the data of revelation with which theology starts is given to it by God through the Church and is not available in usable form from other sources. But other knowledges are not subject to authority in this way. They demand a different attack. It is certainly one of the dangers of being a Catholic that one may never learn to approach natural knowledge on its own terms. Yet dangers exist to be overcome. The challenge to the Catholic here, too, is greater than that to his non-Catholic confreres. For he is called on to live within his own life the tension in terms of which the world is redeemed: that between nature and supernature (which the Greek Fathers call Godlikeness), that between the secular and the sacred, allowing to both realms their own autonomy and effecting the resolution of the tension in his own life in Christ on His cross.

The nineteenth century was a century of intellectual discovery such as the human race had never seen before. Major discovery in the secular sciences, almost inevitably, means that in one way or another the Church will come to a more explicit understanding of the content of the revelation entrusted to her. Meanwhile, as understanding works itself out, certain positions become "dangerous." But a dangerous position can be perfectly true and a "safe" one false and hence in the long run disserviceable to the Church and to religion. In matters relevant even to theology, it is necessary to take some risk, always in submission to the decisions of the Church. For danger is no criterion of truth or falsehood. The holiest mysteries of the faith, that of the Blessed Trinity and of the Incarnation, are dangerous. The one might occasion belief in three gods instead of one God, and the latter might occasion a heretical anthropomorphism. The truths of faith are knife-edged, and we can walk them firmly only with the balance of God's grace in His Church. Living with a certain amount of risk is for the Catholic devoted to the intellectual life, secular or sacred, his own particular share in the cross of Christ.

Index

Abraham, 37, 106
Ahmed Fouad El Ehwany, 137–138
Alfarabius, 137
America, as "land of opportunity," 55–56
American Association of University Professors, 142
American Protective Association, 59
"Americanism," 12
Ames, William, 72
Ancien Régime, 7, 12
Aquinas, St. Thomas, 40, 47, 74, 98, 99, 115, 154
Aristotle, 4–5, 9, 36, 74, 76, 98, 115, 152
Art of Poetry, 4
Auerbach, Erich, 37
Augustine, St., vii–x, 26, 76, 154
Averroës, 137
Avicenna, 137, 138

Baker, Francis A., 48, 53
Basil, St., 76
Bochenski, I. M., O.P., 78
Boehner, Philotheus, O.F.M., 78
Buber, Martin, 34–36, 41

Carlyle, Thomas, 72, 85
Carnap, Rudolf, 79
Catastrophism, 152–154

"Catholic," meaning of, 63–64, 90, 143–144, 151
"Catholic," relationship to learning, 143–144
Christendom, 17–22
Chrysostom, St. John, 76
Church, feminine nature of, 121–124, 128–133; Incarnation and, 3–4; Mystical Body of Christ, 38, 40, 63, 82, 89, 119, 145; state and, 25–45. *See also* Education
Cicero, Marcus Tullius, 20, 115
City of God, City of Man and, vii–x, 8, 15, 26, 29, 44, 50
City of God, St. Augustine's, vii
City of Man. *See* City of God
Clergy, 133–137, 147–149. *See also* Laity
Colleges. *See* Universities and colleges
Communication, as path to truth, 24
Communications, development of, 14
Communism, 7, 59. *See also* Marxism
Comte, Auguste, 20, 82
Confession, dialogic aspect of, 39
Congar, Yves, O.P., 145
Coon, Carleton, 22
Copernicus, Nicolaus, 103
Cosmology, Catholic, present state of, 110–111; Christian, 7
Crombie, A. C., 78

Cullen, Paul, Dr. (later Cardinal), 104
Cullmann, Oscar, 83

Daniélou, Jean, S.J., 83, 145
Darwin, Charles, 81, 85
Dawson, Christopher, 17
Delrio, Martin Antonio, S.J., 96–97
Deshon, George, 48, 53
Dialectic. *See* Dialogue
Dialectical pattern in St. Paul's thinking, 49–53; in John Donne's *Meditations*, 50
Dialectical situation of Paulists, 53–58; of St. Paul, 49–53
Dialogue, American-European, 56–57; in confession, 39; diagrammatic thinking contrasted with, 29–33; dialectic contrasted with, 25–26; love in relation to, 44–45; setting of all human knowledge, 102–103; war and termination of, 44–45
Donne, John, 50

Eck, Johann, 103
Education, Church and differences between elementary, secondary, and higher, 123–128; liberal, 94–96
Einstein, Albert, 11, 100
Eliade, Mircea, 1–2, 5, 6, 83
Eliot, T. S., 111, 127
Erasmus, Desiderius, 127
Eucharist, ix
Evolution, intellectual import of, 98–104
Excommunication, 38–39

Faith (*fides*) and rhetorical tradition, 78
Fanfani, Amintore, 85
Fathers of the Church, vii, ix, 76
Fessard, Gaston, S.J., 53, 77
Frost, Robert, 30

Galilei, Galileo, 102, 107–108
Ganss, George E., S.J., 93
Gelin, Albert, 145
Gibbon, Edward, 15
Gilson, Etienne, 115
Goethe, Johann Wolfgang von, 72

Gospel, preaching of, 17–18, 62
Grace, historicity of, 5–7
Gregory Nazianzen, St., 76
Gregory of Nyssa, St., 76
Guicciardini, Francisco, 9

Hebrews, 4
Hecker, Isaac Thomas, 47–66; dialectical situation of, 53–58, 63
Hegel, Georg Wilhelm Friedrich, 23–25, 32, 82
Heisenberg, Werner, 11
Hewit, Augustine F., 48, 53
Heywood, Jasper, S.J., 103
History, vii–ix, 1–15, 83–89; curial approach to, 7–8; divine Revelation given within, 87–89; human knowledge embedded in, 87–88
Hitler, Adolf, 7
Hobbes, Thomas, 9, 29
Homer, 37, 112
Hopkins, Gerard Manley, S.J., 5
Huxley, Thomas Henry, 154

"I," meaning of, 31; "thou" and, 31–32, 35–36, 39
Ideas, Platonic, 4
Incarnation, 3–6, 10, 14–15, 62, 69, 71, 89, 138, 141
Index of Forbidden Books, 108
Infeld, Leopold, 100
Isidore of Seville, St., 115

Jaspers, Karl, 23–24, 70
Jefferson, Thomas, 9, 30
Jerome, St., 76, 116
Jesus Christ, dialogic and dialectical form of His thinking, 26; history and, 4–5. *See also* Incarnation
Jones, Howard Mumford, 120
Joyce, James, 112

Kazantzakis, Nikos, 112
Khan, Grand, 18
Kierkegaard, Sören, 36, 50
Know-Nothings, 59
Ku Klux Klan, 59
Kublai Khan, 18
Kulturkampf, 7

Index

Laity, 133–134, 149–151. *See also* Clergy
Lamarck, Jean Baptiste, Chevalier de, 152
Lavigerie, Charles Martial Allemand, Cardinal, 12
Leo XIII, Pope, 12
Literature, morality and, 112–113; need for research in, 111–113
Love, dialogue in relation to, 44–45
Loyola, St. Ignatius, 26; dialectic in his *Spiritual Exercises*, 53; rhetoric in his *Spiritual Exercises*, 77
Lubac, Henri de, S.J., 145
Lyell, Sir Charles, 152, 153

Macaulay, Thomas Babington, 15
Macelwane, James B., S.J., 148–149
Mandeville, Sir John, 17
Manicheism, viii
Marcel, Gabriel, 36
Marrou, Henri Irénée, vii, 76
Marx, Karl, 82, 84
Marxism, ix. *See also* Communism
Mary, Mother of God, ix, 6
Mendel, Gregor, 103
Miller, Perry, viii
Missionary Society of St. Paul the Apostle (Paulists), 48–58, 62, 65–66. *See also* Hecker, Isaac Thomas
Modernists, 10
Moody, Ernest A., 78
Movius, Hallam L., Jr., 111
Mussolini, Benito, 7
Mustafa Abd El Razik, 138
Mystical Body of Christ. *See* Church

Names (nouns) in dialogue, use of, 31–32
Napoleon, 7
Natural sciences, need for research in, 115
Nature (*natura*) as birth, 3, 70, 85
Nestorians, 17
Newman, John Henry, Cardinal, 15, 54, 83, 104, 119, 127–128, 135
Newton, Sir Isaac, 72
Nouns. *See* Names

Pasteur, Louis, 154
Paul, St., vii, 5, 18, 26, 27, 48–59, 62, 65; dialectical pattern of his thought, 49–53, 65
Paulists. *See* Missionary Society of St. Paul the Apostle
Perkins, William, 72
Person, Church and, 37–45; dialogue and, 31–32; dogmatic interest in, 40–41; object versus, 31–32; state and, 33–45
Peter, St., 54
Philosophy, need for research in, 110–111
Planck, Max, 10
Plato (Platonism), 4–5, 9, 76
Poetry, history and, 4
Polo, Marco, 17–18
Prayer, dialogic quality of, 28; rhetoric and, 76–78
Prometheus, 4
Pronouns, in dialogue, use of, 31–32
Protestants, American, viii
Ptolemy, 152
Puritan tradition, viii

Ralliement, 12
Ramus, Peter (Petrus Ramus, Pierre de la Ramée), 29–30
Redemption, 15
Religion, nationalism and, 20; "organized," 41
Revolution, French, 7
Riesman, David, 85
Rougemont, Denis de, 28, 40
Rousseau, Jean Jacques, 20
Russell, Bertrand, 79

Sartre, Jean Paul, 32
Seneca, Lucius Annaeus, 96–97, 103
Social sciences, need for research in, 113–114
Society of Jesus, 97
Socrates, 76
Spencer, Herbert, 153
Spitzer, Leo, 71
Stanford, W. B., 112
Steensen, Niels, 153
Stern, Karl, 11

Tawney, R. H., 85
Teilhard de Chardin, Pierre, S.J., 22, 110–111
Theology, need for research in, 107
Time, Catholic sense of, 5–7; cyclic and other, 83–84

Ulysses, 112
United States of America, ix
"Universal," narrower than "Catholic," 63–64
Universe, time and space in, 9–10

Universities, American compared with European, 93–98
Universities and colleges, organization of American, 142–143

Vitoria, Francisco de, O.P., 102

Wallace, Alfred Russel, 81
Weber, Max, 85
Whitehead, Alfred North, 73–74, 79
Williams, Roger, 7
Wreck of the Deutschland, The, 5